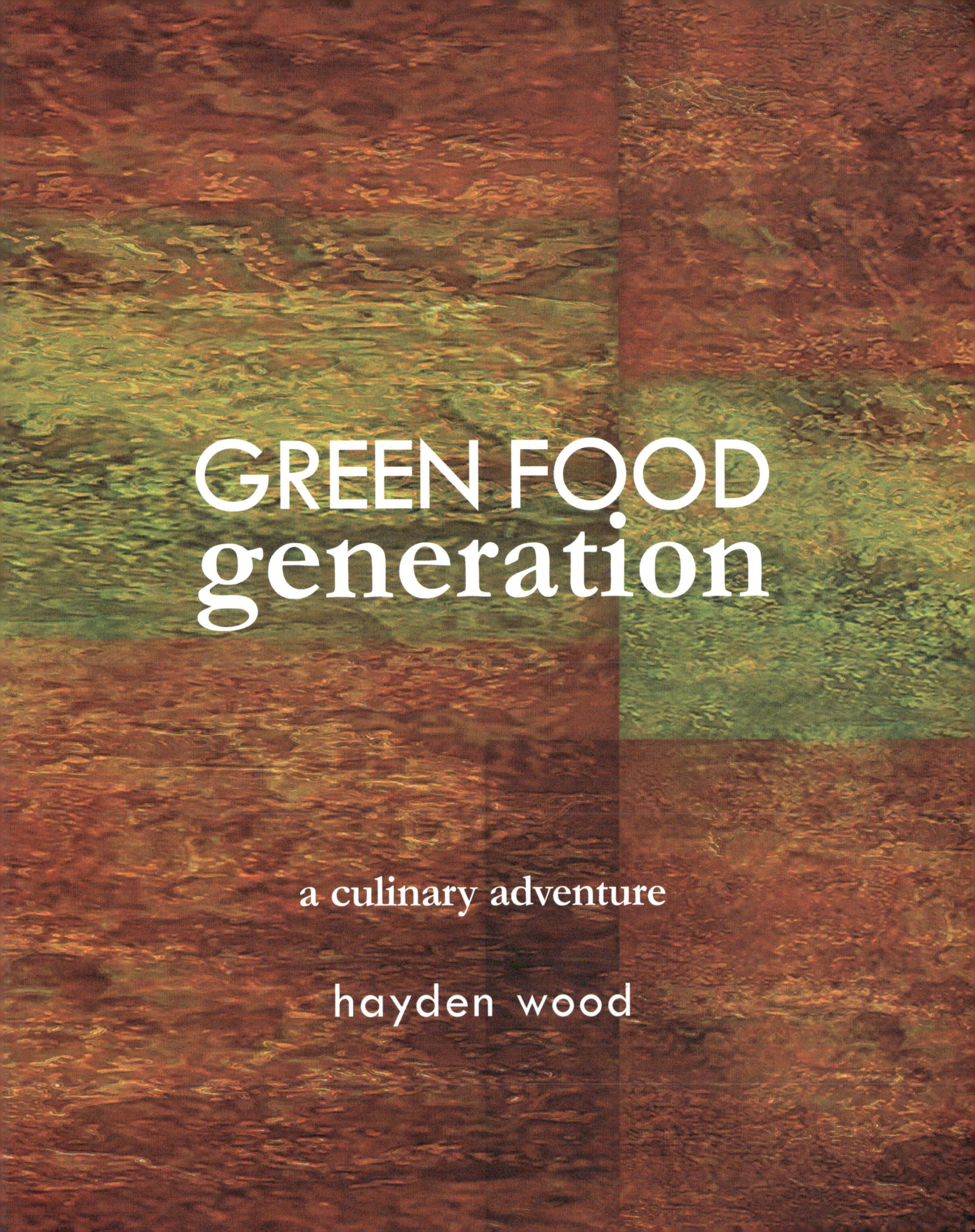

GREEN FOOD
generation

a culinary adventure

hayden wood

For my brother Sam
and your return to the land after a full circle

Contents

Foreword — *8*

Green Food Generation — *11*

A Culinary Adventure — *15*
My Dad - Russell Wood — *18*
Russell's Homemade Camembert Cheese and Vivvy's Flower Pot Bread — *20*

Oz Harvest — *23*
OzHarvest's Recipe for Feeding People — *28*

Bird Cow Fish — *31*
Crooked Madame — *36*

VictorsFood — *39*
Devilish Tequila Prawns — *44*

Gastronomy — *49*
Organic Chicken and Tarragon Consommé and Tortellini — *54*

Selah Restaurant — *57*
Olive Oil Poached Atlantic Salmon with Shaved Fennel, Shiso and Sevillano Olive Salad with Candied Orange and Confit Tomato Dressing — *62*

Courtney's Brasserie — *65*
Courtney's Beef Bourguignon — *70*

Hungry Duck — 73
Sashimi of Local Line-Caught Fish with
Lemon, Lime and Fresh Horseradish or Wasabi — 78

Bells at Killcare Boutique Hotel Restaurant and Bar — 81
Mushroom Frittatina Rolls with Salsa Verde — 86

Margan Family Winegrowers and Restaurant and Tasting Room — 91
Seared Pepper-Crusted Kingfish
and Crispy Silverbeet with Anchovy Mayonnaise — 96

Racine @ La Colline — 99
Venison with Spring Pea Purée and Soft Boiled Quail's Egg — 104

La Table Café and Restaurant — 107
Duck Confit with Five Spice and Shiraz Sauce — 112

South Bank Surf Club — 115
Wasabi Prawns in Angel Hair with Mango and Watermelon Salad — 120

Ochre Restaurant and Catering — 125
Salt and Pepperleaf Prawns and Crocodile with
Vietnamese Pickles, Lemon Aspen Sambal — 130

Saffrron Restaurant — 133
Barramundi Varvul — 138

Grumpy's Green — 141
Grumpy's Green Nepalese Chickpea and Red Lentil Dhal — 146

Spice Island *149*
Dukkah and Crispy Thrice-Cooked Quail *154*

Stefano's Café Bakery *157*
Yabbies and Sausage Scrambled Eggs *162*

d'Arry's Verandah Restaurant *167*
Beetroot Cake with Hindmarsh Valley Goat Curd Dumpling *172*

The Brasserie at Hilton Adelaide *175*
Pepper Berry and Bush Tomato-Rubbed Kangaroo Saddle with Warrigal Greens and Muntries, Crispy Saltbush and Quandong and Desert Lime Glaze *180*

The Source Restaurant at Mona *183*
Broiled Oysters with Seaweed Emulsion and Buckwheat Velouté *188*

The FIG Cafés *191*
Ooey Gooey with Honey Balsamic Figs *196*

Green Food Glossary *199*

Acknowledgments *202*

Thank You *203*

Recipe Index *206*

foreword

by Curtis Stone

As a chef I'm often quizzed on which other chefs I admire or might look up to most. While I love eating the food of all kinds of chefs, I have to tell you that I think we've got the easy job. It's the food producers of the world that really have their work cut out for them.

In a world where food's becoming more and more processed, it's increasingly more difficult for REAL food producers to compete. I'll never forget when I was about twenty five or twenty six years old: I was lucky enough to work on a television series where we travelled all around Australia and got to meet all sorts of food producers, from mango growers to mussel farmers, crab fishermen and pig farmers. What really struck me was that the more a producer cared for their ingredient - and I really mean the more love and passion they had for what they did - the better it tasted.

Actually, here's a list of what I reckon it takes to produce great food: Love, Respect, Understanding, Patience, Care, Passion, Responsibility, Water, Sunshine, Time

It's funny to write a list like this out, but imagine if we all lived with more of these qualities in our day to day lives? How does the saying go? "You are what you eat?"

By that logic, we're all better off eating well-produced food, right?

You might ask "Well, what is well-produced food or green food or even natural food, for that matter?"

And these are really good questions as these days words like "natural" and "green" are unfortunately pretty over-used.

My answer is: green food is food that's responsibly produced. It's food production with a conscience. I ask all food producers I meet: "is this something you'd be happy to serve to your family?"

At the end of the day there aren't too many things that many of us like more than gathering round the table with family and friends to enjoy a delicious spread of great food and good wine. It sounds clichéd, but the simple things in life really are the best.

Which in my mind is absolutely why REAL food always tastes so much better.

While I might have grown up working in Michelin-starred restaurants, I've always believed that the key to great cuisine starts with great ingredients. Mother Nature did a pretty amazing job supplying us with an abundant selection of ingredients for all seasons.

So when it comes to cooking, my philosophy's always been to cook as Mother Nature intended: buy locally produced, seasonal and organic ingredients - and allow the food to speak for itself.

You know, it's funny to look back and remember when I met Hayden Wood (aka Woody) for the first time around ten years ago. You could say we had a few things in common: I mean, the guy can chew an ear or two, and I'm pretty much the same when it comes to yacking about all things foodie. So yes, there was some rapturous banter, and naturally running into each other on the good food show circuit, we soon became great mates. We've also developed the convenient habit of bumping into each other at various locations around the globe: Australia, New Zealand, or in more recent times, the United States.

Woody's a natural entertainer and has the knack of getting a crowd pumping in a heartbeat. His passion and drive for all things food and beverage makes him the perfect person to champion a culinary adventure that showcases the cooks and characters that support our green and sustainable philosophies. In his quest to soak up green culture Woody celebrates the inspiring individuals that are the cornerstones of the green food scene.

While a great percentage of the population has become accustomed to purchasing meals that are ready to consume with the mere press of a microwave button, there's a whole culture out there trying to slow it all down, grow locally and develop sustainable and ethical farming practices. Woody's culinary travelogue reveals some of these guardians of Mother Nature dotted around Australia and New Zealand who are trying to preserve these important culinary traditions.

Wouldn't you agree that food that's in season just tastes so much better? And that food that hasn't been drastically tampered with or carted half-way across the world is so much better for you and the environment? It's an amazing responsibility all of us have in the food industry, but it's such an important one. Supporting regional culinary traditions and produce really is one of many steps to paving the way to help improve our understanding of what we should eat and when. Encouraging people to entertain with a conscience and take the time to celebrate what's naturally on offer is one of life's many great pleasures… and one we should all continue to embrace and enjoy!

Green Food Generation

The Green Food revolutionaries I met on this culinary adventure represent a small but strong generation of the chefs, farmers, fishermen and other producers that make up the growing Green Food revolution in Australia. They're as generous with their time as they are enthusiastic about good, fresh, great-tasting food, and they've served up a cornucopia of stories and recipes that I hope will inspire generations of readers and cooks to expect as much of their food and food producers as these passionate green foodies are.

We've seen over the past few years how non-sustainable, commercially-produced food has become more and more of an issue for all of us. Factory farming, genetically- and chemically-modified food, unsustainable "food miles," "affluence diseases" like allergies, heart disease, diabetes and obesity have all come to the fore for discerning cooks, shoppers and parents.

Yet, for many of us, it's all a bit too hard. Isn't green food hippy food? Isn't it all nut roast and lentils, served up on a steaming bed of self-righteousness? Not according to the passionate and creative people you'll meet here: as they prove over and over again, food that's good for you and good for the planet can taste good too.

Still, only a sustainable business can keep dishing up sustainable food, and while these outstanding restaurants, cafés, bars and caterers continue to attract new and dedicated followers, they also appreciate that although it's not always easy being green, you can have a good time trying! Nothing's perfect, and everyone you'll meet acknowledge that sometimes it's not always possible to always source locally, or organically, or with minimum emissions.

Green Food Generation doesn't try to 'Green Wash' anything. All the people you'll meet face many challenges to their commitment to a sustainable food supply and all of them would like to be doing more and better at what they already are achieving. But they all try to do what they can, and it's from little seeds big things grow.

I started out on my green food adventure on New Zealand's magnificent South Island, where I spent some great days with my family on their wonderful Geraldine farm. To go back to where it all began for me was an important part of this culinary journey as I'd be applying what I learned from spending this precious family time back home in Sydney.

It was from here the seed was sown. From there, I found talented chefs and amazing personalities all over the country eager to tell their stories, share their ideas and recipes, and offer a taste of their own amazing green food adventures, taking me along to meet equally dedicated producers and introducing me to their delicious food and inspiring philosophies.

It wasn't just educational: it was exciting! To see what this energetic, engaged green food generation had to offer was an extraordinary experience, and I'm grateful to all of them. It was as if I'd finally shaken the cocktail goggles from my eyes: although I'd enjoyed the hospitality of a number of these fantastic places before, I'd never really thought about all the tremendous work done behind the scenes to ensure that the cuisine I was enjoying didn't just taste great, but was great for the environment and the community. Of course, you don't need to know everything that goes on behind kitchen doors, but having an idea of the effort and care that goes on between the farmer's gate and your plate will hopefully inspire you to start your own green food revolution.

We may not save the world on our own, but if we can work together, raising awareness and demanding the best, we just might do it.

I know, looking at our beautiful son Zyon, that it's worth the effort. And the best thing is that it's not that hard at all!

I hope you don't just enjoy meeting these wonderful people, or trying their amazing recipes, or visiting their amazing establishments, but that like me, you too are inspired to ask some simple questions, do some small things, and expect as much of your food as you and your family deserve. It's only by asking for the sustainable, locally-produced, free-range, organic, bio-dynamic and passionately served food that I call "Green Food" that we can let our chefs and grocers and food producers know to make the very best food for us, and for the planet.

Hayden Wood aka "Woody"

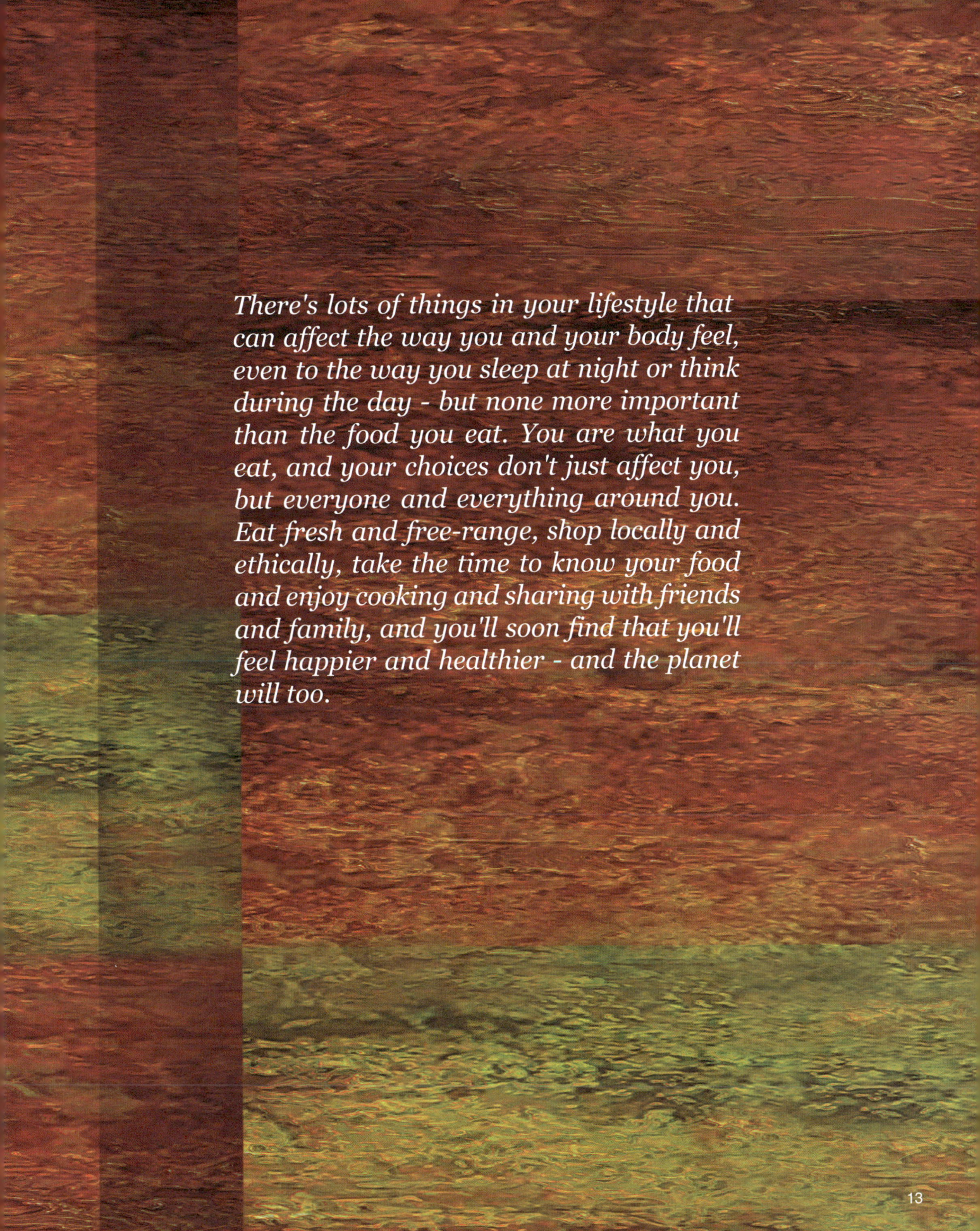

There's lots of things in your lifestyle that can affect the way you and your body feel, even to the way you sleep at night or think during the day - but none more important than the food you eat. You are what you eat, and your choices don't just affect you, but everyone and everything around you. Eat fresh and free-range, shop locally and ethically, take the time to know your food and enjoy cooking and sharing with friends and family, and you'll soon find that you'll feel happier and healthier - and the planet will too.

A Culinary Adventure

Hayden Wood, aka "Woody"

This is me. As a flair cocktail bartender, I've toured the world. Recently, I had a fun, frenzied, fantastic time touring the United States, whirling and pouring on a rock n' roll food-apalooza for thousands of people in a different city every night. Actually, it's called food theatre over there, and until now - along with designing exciting cocktails for some of the world's coolest and biggest parties - it's enabled me to indulge in my passion for great food and drink of all kinds, publishing coffee table books on the best cocktails, wine, beer and coffee Australia, New Zealand and the world have to offer.

And it's also given me countless wonderful opportunities to experience some very different and exotic cultures and cuisines, and to meet lots of amazing and talented chefs, bartenders, winemakers, brewers, foodies and fans. And it's all thanks to them and their generous encouragement, I've found myself in the enviable position of being able to now embark on the kind of culinary adventures I love to share with friends, family and readers.

Just as Americans love great cocktails, they love food. Lots of food.

Although my waistline didn't appreciate the abundance, I loved how surprisingly varied and rich American cuisine was. It isn't just all-you-can-eat buffets, oversized burgers and junk food: I loved discovering regional specialities, respectfully preserved and lovingly prepared. New England clam chowder, Philly cheesesteak, Cajun jambalaya … the menu goes on and on. And I'm not even going to get into where you can find the best slice!

What I especially loved was how passionate people were about their food: where to find the best pancakes, the best pizza, the best fries or dogs. Every town had their own special diner and own dining speciality, and enjoying all the hospitality my enthusiastic hosts had to offer, I found my interest in cocktails was matched by my new interest in eating new and local food.

But America is a diverse country, and its cuisine, with the ingredients of the many different influences of its immigrants and immediate neighbours, has made them its own: German frankfurters became hotdogs, Jewish bagels reubens, and the spice of Central and South American cuisines Tex-Mex: stirring everything into a great melting-pot of colour and flavour.

Of course, it's easy to forget, cruising another strip-mall filled with fast-food chains selling the same old deep-fried cheesy same old. Not to mention the immense problems of obesity, diabetes, heart disease, food allergies and more. But thanks to public health programmes there, people are starting to become more aware, and best of all, are starting to get some new and healthy options.

Whether it was organic farmers' markets, low-sugar or salt options in the supermarket aisle, or even calorie and nutrition information on hamburger wrappers, it was a positive sign that people just want the facts, so that they can really make the right choice, no matter how many flavours there are!

But as one of America's leading celebrity chefs, Guy Fieri will tell you, obesity isn't caused by a soda machine at junior high - rather, it's not taking the time to cook and eat together as a family. We live busier and busier lives, rushing from school to work to everything in between, but the bad eating habits and worse health of an entire generation can be found in the half-defrosted leftovers of convenience food and TV dinners. Our crazy food culture, which throws bigger and beefier portions at us while casting disapproving glances at our cellulite has contributed to children today being the first generation ever to have a lower life expectancy than its parents.

Guy's mantra to change the way the whole country cooks and eats is to start with the family.

'Cooking dinner together as a family is a critical way to learn about food and to know what's going in to your body,'

he once told me. 'We don't really know what's gone into most packaged food, or even where it's been.'

It got me thinking: you wouldn't pick up a sandwich someone had left on the footpath, so why would you eat food you didn't know anything about? What had I been eating lately that I didn't know anything about? What had I been eating? It really gave me the "willies." And very serious pause for thought.

Suddenly, I started to notice there were two very distinct food cultures: the one we're most familiar with, now "new and improved" with added convenience, lashings of deluxe disco-coloured advertising, and wrapped up in garish "stay-fresh" packaging, distracting us from the cryptic fine print on the back of the label. You know, flavour enhancers 621, 635, 632 or colouring agents 155, E143, 161h. What the heck is anti-caking agent, anyhow? And how good for you can sodium propyl p-hydroxybenzoate be for you (as it turns out, not very)?

Then there's that brave group of people who seek out food produced by the earth, not factories; who seek out food that's organic, bio-dynamic, free-range, sustainable. Up until recently, it seems, these terms were only intelligible to hippies and ferals who didn't "buy into the system, man."

After all, how easy is it to grow your own veggies when you live on a commune and don't have a job? Have you seen the traffic in a big city lately? Do you know how hard it is to come up with good food when you don't have time to scratch, let alone shop or cook?

I was born and raised on a farm, so while I do understand the importance of the care that goes into food before it reaches our plates, as a busy bon vivant and parent, I also know the demands of time and energy that involve getting it there to feed impatient, hungry tummies!

This paradox came up a lot in my 15, 000 kilometre journey around the country. Again and again, the simple reply was:

support farmers' markets, buy more natural and much less packaged food.

Of course, by doing this, you'll naturally cook more from scratch, and in turn, your local farmers, providores and suppliers will have enough demand to supply more. It's a growing thing: as you wow your friends and family with your great tasting good food, they'll be inspired to try as well. And, when you think about it, rather than recycling your empty plastic food packaging, why not just do away with it altogether, using the compostable scraps for your worm farm or garden? Green Food, as I call it (and, of course, the book) is organic, bio-dynamic, free-range, sustainable, good for you, good for the planet, and growing every day in popularity and prominence.

But I didn't start on this journey to highlight the problems. Rather,

I wanted to celebrate the achievements of what I call "the Green Food Generation."

I was so excited by the energy and enthusiasm of these talented, passionate people, I felt kinda guilty about forgetting my sound start in life. So to get the wind in my sails before I set out on this green food adventure, I jumped a carbon-neutral seat to Christchurch, New Zealand, where it all began for me, and hung out with my dad,

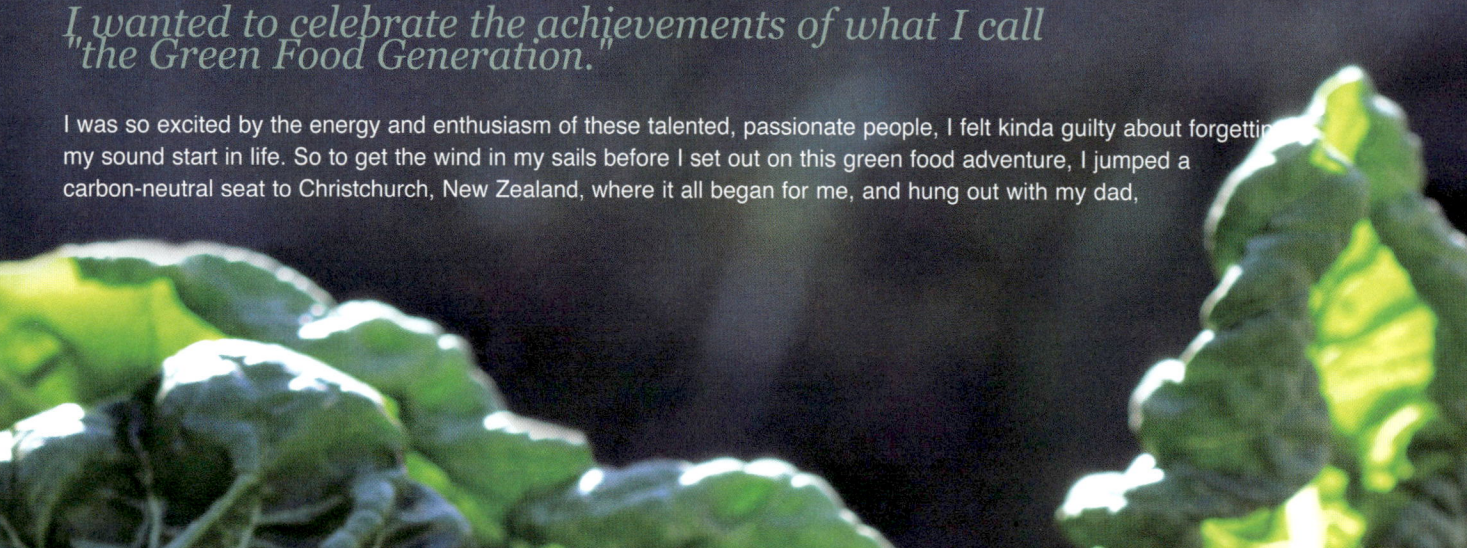

My Dad - Russell Wood
aka "Gandalf the Green"

My dad isn't your average dad, exactly, but hey, who's comparing? We call him Gandalf the Green because he lives in the foothills of the South Island's magnificent Tolkienesque mountains, and he's the epitome of self sufficiency and sustainability.

He's the most passionate and knowledgeable person living a green life I know. His active involvement in nurturing and fostering a sustained future as a volunteer for local salmon hatcheries means he knows as much, if not more, than anybody about the state of both sea and river fisheries and fishing grounds. He's been a farmer for as long as I can remember, and if there's something he doesn't know about raising chickens, sheep, cattle, deer, pigs, goats, dairy cows or any other farm animal - well, his neighbours will gladly trade a slice of smoked salmon or two for any answers he needs.

Just as he did when I was growing up, Gandalf - I mean, Dad - still keeps an extensive vegetable garden growing a rich and wide variety of the earthiest spuds, sweet potatoes, vibrant pumpkins, delicious carrots, snap-fresh beans and the sweetest peas you'll ever taste. Leafy cabbage and lush lettuce patches are flanked by citrus trees and yam beds.

In the sustainable greenhouse, there's juicy tomatoes, refreshing cucumbers, plump strawberries and a fragrant herb garden. It's a green food wonderland!

And that's only the start of it - space precludes me from mentioning all the other fresh, natural food the farm produces on its rich, fertile soil. But in the freezer, you'll find an abundant harvest of wild game, including rabbit, hare, venison, Canadian goose, wild boar, line-caught river salmon and rainbow trout, and anything else Dad has managed to forage, find, fish or swap for his prized free range roosters.

When I dropped by, Dad took me to his river batch, or holiday house, down on the Rangatata River mouth to go wild salmon fishing. Although I came home empty-handed, I left gorged on pristine fresh air, Vivvy's homemade strawberry jam pancakes, hot tea and precious father-and-son time in one of the world's most breathtaking and remote places.

The next morning, we rose at five in the morning to make it up the road to a local organic dairy farm for milking. It was snowing, and Bryan, Dad's farmer mate, cooked up a wonderful organic milk and yoghurt porridge for us to enjoy over sunrise. We started talking about the A2 protein found in organic dairy food, which some studies have shown can lower heart disease, autism and adult-onset diabetes risks in children, as well as being beneficial for people suffering from allergies, immune deficiencies or digestive disorders.

Bryan reckoned that all plants needed to be put under some pressure or stress during growth to release vitamins and nutrients like that of the A2 protein found in milk. Unfortunately, the demands of higher yields and more frequent harvests meant technology like hydroponics, hot-housing, pesticiding and cold-transport had meant that while production volumes had increased, the chemically and sometimes genetically engineered and controlled food that was produced lacked those important nutrients - or, as everybody around the table agreed, that wonderful taste.

Those barely red tomatoes and oversized strawbs might have made the long journey from agri-business to you relatively and uniformly intact, but what had we lost in the process? Everybody knew that the best way to get the vitamins and minerals you needed for a long and healthy life was to eat fresh fruit and veggies, but if that was the case, why did so many otherwise healthy people need so many vitamin supplements nowadays?

Nutritional education aside, the big thing I discovered spending some time with Dad and his neighbours was that taking it a little slower and lavishing a little extra care to our food, our bodies and our communities offers far richer rewards than any half-eaten sanger thrown down at our desks. Regardless of how many celebrity chefs on the tube, or how much we talk about the "finest" products flown in from half a world away, all we really need is where it always was: right under our noses.

Good, fresh, locally produced food doesn't just feed a family: it nourishes a community.

Sure, sometimes you won't be able to get that exotic ingredient locally, but the more you do try to buy locally, the more likely it is that your favourite provedore will be able to supply a local version one day - you just have to support them, and ask!

Dad and I talked a lot about what values were placed on food in our hectic, urbanized culture. How important was nourishment, not just of the body, but the palate - and even the soul? Or was it simply fuel to get us from one meeting to the next? Something quick to fill the aching pang, perhaps? 'I wouldn't know, son,' said Dad, helping himself to more of his garden's bounty. 'But I'm not having anything to do with that sort of stuff.'

One man's pleasure is another man's poison, goes the old saying, and what food is and means is different to each and every one of us. But what is it to us as a community, as a country, as a culture? Getting home and grabbing those plastic wrapped supermarket veggies and that sterile vacuum-packed meat, I couldn't help but wonder if desensitising us about where our food really comes from isn't just part of the problem, but the problem itself. After all, despite what the kids might think, they don't farm meat in silly shapes or from meat trays, do they? Do they?

Dad laughs. "Now, that's another can of worms,' he says. 'Or meat tray…'

After all the brain pain produced by trying to solve all the world's problems one meat tray at a time over a bottle of his powerful home brew, he gets me in the kitchen to learn how to make cheese, while Vivvy baked her famous flower pot bread.

We might only be at the start of our great green food quest, but you couldn't take better provisions than Gandalf's camembert, brie, blue vein and cheddar, homemade with Brian's delicious, organic, raw whole milk, which we'd helped milk ourselves, slathered on Vivvy's light flower pot bread, could you?

Russell's Homemade Camembert Cheese and Vivvy's Flower Pot Bread

serves four as an entrée

Never thought you could make your own cheese? Think again! Enjoy this homemade creamy camembert with flower pot bread for a simple, melt-in-your-mouth snack. Keep in mind you can easily add ingredients such as herbs, fruit, nuts and seeds to enjoy your flower pot bread any way you like. Russell loves his with sunflower and I love it with pumpkin seeds - but the beauty is you can make it any way you like. You could even go the whole hog and make it part of a delicious ploughman's lunch!

A great place to start is www.greenlivingaustralia.com.au , where you can purchase the Type E starter and camembert mould spores used in the recipe.

Russell loves it with his favourite homebrewed lager or Central Otago pinot noir. Whatever you drink with it, whatever way you enjoy it, just make sure you have good company!

ingredients

Gandalf's Homemade Camembert
10L milk (organic, preferably, of course!)
¼ teaspoons camembert starter
2.5ml rennet
¼ teaspoons camembert mould spores

Vivvy's Flower Pot Bread
500ml home brew beer, preferably lager
3 cups organic wholemeal flour
1 cup grated cheese of your choice
3 teaspoons baking powder
1 teaspoons salt
garlic, herbs, spices, seeds to taste

method

Gandalf's Homemade Camembert
Heat pasteurised milk gently to 35°C. Add camembert starter, rennet and mould spores. Leave to set in pot for 40 minutes

Cut curd into 2cm cubes using a long bread knife. Rest for 30 minutes, then turn curd squares over gently for 3 minutes continuously. Leave for another 30 minutes. Remove as much of the whey that can be strained from the pot using the pot lid to retain the curds. Using a sieve to remove the curds and strain excess whey, place remaining curds and whey into hoops or cheese moulds (around 100ml high and 150ml in diameter) that allow the whey to drain from the curds. You could pack into cheese cloth and mould into a cake tin with holes in its base or a small sieve. While resting, the curds must be on a free draining matt like a bamboo sushi rolling matt.

Turn over cheeses after 30 minutes. Leave overnight on cake racks in a large plastic tub in a humid place, like your pantry or kitchen cupboard, for mould to grow. Next day, soak for 15 minutes in brine solution (2 parts salt to 8 parts water). Return to humid place for mould to grown on the outside and check once every second day to release some humidity, as you'll also need a little fresh air every now and then. This may take two to three days. Be patient! Maturation may take up to 1 week.

Wrap each cheese in baking paper and store in fridge for up to 3 weeks. Be careful when making two different kinds of cheese - say, blue vein and camembert - to use separate utensils and pots to avoid contamination.

Vivvy's Flower Pot Bread
Preheat oven to 200°C. Put all dry ingredients into a bowl then mix in beer to make dough.

Get a clean unused 1L terracotta flower pot (although after first use the pot can be used time and time again) and liberally rub the inside with butter and also cover the hole in the base with baking paper. Then line with seasoning, herbs, spices, and a little flower.

Spoon dough into flower pot. Top extra grated cheese, herbs, and seeds. Bake for 35 to 40 minutes until risen and golden. Tip out of flower pot and cool on a baking rack. Serve with homemade butter, cheese and pickles.

Oz Harvest
Ronni Kahn

As anyone who's ever worked in hospitality and catering will tell you, it's gut-wrenching seeing mountains of delicious and perfectly edible food just being thrown out at the end of the day. What a Waste - An Analysis of Household Expenditure on Food, a 2009 report by the Australia Institute, found that Australian households throw away a staggering $5.2 billion of food a year - more than the nation's entire military budget! The figures from industry dwarf that, with not only massive amounts of money being chucked into the bin, but frightening environmental impacts as well, from greenhouse gas emissions and water use in production, transportation and disposal; and Australia's already overwhelmed landfill sites clogged to overflowing with the 1.1 million tonnes of the rotting food that comprises over a third of weekly garbage - and all the vermin and disease that attracts.

The worst part is that even in a First World nation like the Lucky Country, there are so many people who need that food to survive, especially in the wake of the worst financial crisis the world has ever seen.

Having worked in hospitality for over twenty years, Ronni Kahn was devastated by the enormous waste produced by the hospitality industry. After first hand experience and extensive research into how excess food was collected and disposed of, she discovered that there was no organisation that had the mission, let alone capacity, to collect and redistribute that food in a systematic way. With all the passion and energy which she'd become such a success in event production, Ronni founded OzHarvest in 2004, Australia's first food redistribution charity, working closely with OzHarvest's many wonderful volunteers, other charities and generous restaurants, hotels and catering companies to bring some of Sydney's best food to some of its neediest people. Is it any wonder Ronni, OzHarvest's Founding Director and CEO, is also a 2010 Australian of the Year Local Hero?

Just how much food does OzHarvest donate?
We donate over 6,000 meals a day to over 190 recipient agencies, thanks to the generosity of over 900 donors and the hard work of hundreds of volunteers. It costs less than a single dollar to ensure someone doesn't go hungry tonight. And we've got lots of exciting new programs and events, including Feed Sydney, Cooking for a Cause, and Cooking for a Cause to find Love!

Singles' Cooking Classes?
Yeah! [laughs] What we're doing is inviting 250 of Sydney's hottest singles to get together, learn to make some awesome food, have fun and hopefully meet the person of their dreams - someone with the same culinary flair and generous heart! And best of all, OzHarvest will donate whatever they make to needy people that very night! We'll prepare at least 5,000 meals from that one event.

That's just mind-blowing! But we live in the Lucky Country! Are that many meals really needed?
Yes, they are! We already provide 6,000 meals a day, collecting more than twelve tonnes of surplus food per week that's already been produced for consumption - and that's just in Sydney. And we could provide much more if we had the resources - we currently have six vans and a truck, but you can just imagine how many more meals are needed and how much food's being wasted throughout Australia!

You deal with so much food from so many donors for so many people. What do you cook when you get home?
Fresh, organic, local produce. For me, the best food's simple, beautiful, fresh, tasty and uncomplicated. I don't stock up when I buy, but just what I need that day for that particular dish, and I try to avoid the supermarket - I'm lucky I have a wonderful fruit shop and deli where I live, which I support enthusiastically. I believe in green food philosophies like sustainability and limiting food miles, and even if unfortunately you can't always tick every box in one hit, I do try my best.

Funnily enough, though, while consumers have become much more aware about the environmental impact of the food they buy, they just don't seem to think that much about the massive waste they produce. And they're both related - there's just as much energy wasted in transporting waste as there is in transporting food: and that awareness and conscientiousness, starting with what you buy, needs to go to the obvious conclusion and end with what you put in the bin, or better, in the compost.

Do you factor in food miles for your collection and delivery?
Well, we're very mindful. We deliver food to the same areas we collect from. When an OzHarvest van goes out in one direction, it collects food on its way and delivers it en route. We're looking at greener options for our truck and vans and minimising our carbon footprint, but we've also saved the equivalent of thousands of cars' emissions, just by having saved thousands of tonnes of good food from being transported to landfill and polluting the atmosphere and soil. Still, every little bit helps, doesn't it?

Having had a lot of experience of catered events myself, I've seen heaps of food being thrown out. How did you go from "that's a shame" to changing your life's work?
I used to run an event production company. Most of our events revolved around good food and because we had to plan against any shortages, there'd always be waste. I used to drop off what surplus food I could to an agency on my way home, but I could never deliver enough - it was always easier to just turf it into the bin. It just broke my heart, especially thinking of all the people who needed it and could use it. The main thing about OzHarvest isn't just helping people who need it, it's also making individuals and businesses aware of the immense, needless waste that can be put to good use, rather than clogging landfill. There's always been waste and there always will be, just as there have always been people in need and there unfortunately always will be. So we're trying to do something about it - to create awareness and make sure this food doesn't go to waste. There's no doubt at all that this is my life's work, my life's purpose - and I'm glad I can do something. I'd like to do more!

What's your pet hate about the food industry?
Overproduction without any thought or care for the planet. And there's no awareness or desire to share mass production of food amongst everybody.

Why should one billion people in the world - including nine million in the so-called "developed world" - not have enough to eat, and 25,000 people - most of them little children - die every single day from starvation, when so much food thoughtlessly goes to waste,

or when massive "surplus" piles of grain go to waste in silos in America and Europe?

Do you think that population growth has contributed to those food issues of starvation and waste?

No, not at all. We're plundering our planet without any thought or regard for those less fortunate or in the so-called Third World. For example, the Asia-Pacific's home to half the world's population and two-thirds of its starving people, with more than 65% living in seven countries: India, China, Bangladesh, Indonesia, Pakistan, the Democratic Republic of Congo and Ethiopia. So, it's not a question of resources, but resource management and exploitation.

The West spends US$230 million a day fighting in Afghanistan alone; yet the few hundred million dollars the UN has asked for fighting starvation seem very hard to come by. Where's the logic or compassion in that?

Everybody's parents tell them "there are starving kids in India" but if we put ourselves in their shoes, how would we feel if we were starving, knowing people just threw away without a second thought the food that could save us or our children? Next time you do waste your food, just think of those people - and try to do something about it. You might not be able to donate or volunteer - although it'd be great if you could - but just thinking about what you waste as much as what you eat can make a difference.

Do you plan on expanding beyond Sydney, Canberra and Wollongong?

Of course! We're working on expanding to Adelaide, where we had the food donation laws recently changed to enable good food from food outlets such as hotels, restaurants and caterers to be donated to South Australia's homeless and needy. We'll be able to rescue the thousands of tonnes of edible food that would have otherwise been thrown away. After that, hopefully Brisbane, then Perth, it just depends on where the money comes from and how quickly it comes...

Venue

OzHarvest's food is donated by some of Australia's biggest and best caterers, function centres, hotels, wholesalers, retailers, restaurants, cafés, delis, supermarkets and more. Some of OzHarvest's biggest donors are supermarkets such as ALDI and Woolworths, regularly donating the fresh food, fruit and vegetables that many disadvantaged people cannot afford. Two other great donors are the incredibly popular and renowned Bourke Street Bakery and Central Baking Depot, whose generous staffs' regular tweets of their love for OzHarvest reflect the organisation's close relationship with its 900 donors.

Other donors include Gastronomy, Sydney's biggest and best catering company; major hotels like Four Seasons International, Hilton International, Intercontinental and Crowne Plaza Hotels; and some of Sydney's coolest restaurants and cafés, like Danks Street Depot, Bill's, Bertoni Casalinga, Firefly, Malaya and more. And some of Australia's biggest corporations and organisations have shown their social consciences, including the Macquarie Foundation, Goodman+ (who donated OzHarvest's first van and office space), the city's biggest law firms, major banks, its best schools, Government departments and unions. But it's the help and generosity of hundreds of small, unsung heroes, like Chargrill Charlies at Mosman, Rose Bay's Grandma Moses or Vivo's in the CBD which make as much of a difference. Together, we can all do our bit to share the responsibility of ensuring that all Australians can enjoy the basic goodness we all deserve. After all, as OzHarvest proves day in, day out, we're only as rich as our poorest, as strong as our weakest, and as well-fed as our hungriest fellow Australians.

If you're wondering about food donation and the possible legal liabilities, OzHarvest lobbied to have the groundbreaking NSW Civil Liability Amendment (Food Donations) Act 2005 No 16, which indemnified donors from legal liability, a major stumbling block for donation in the past. Other States and Territories, including the ACT, Queensland,

South Australia and soon Western Australia, have all passed similar legislation thanks to OzHarvest's efforts, opening the door for OzHarvest to expand to those States, contingent on the generosity of food donors, financial supporters and volunteers.

If you'd like to donate food, time or money to OzHarvest, check out their website at http://www.ozharvest.org.au/index.asp for more information.

Food and Ingredients

OzHarvest's mission to redistribute some of Australia's best food to some of Australia's neediest people has been a runaway environmental and humanitarian success, collecting over 7 000 meals a day for some of Sydney, Canberra and Wollongong's neediest people at a cost of only a dollar a meal - all perfectly good food from some of Australia's best restaurants and events that would have otherwise just been thrown away to rot in landfill. Soon expanding to other State capitals, its impact can only grow, with much more food saved and many more people fed.

Despite the massive amount of meals they collect and distribute from over 900 donors to over 200 recipient agencies, OzHarvest runs on a small team of passionate staff and dedicated volunteers 'who are absolutely pivotal,' says Ronni gratefully. From driving to delivering, sourcing new food donors and helping in the office, it's their generosity and energy that helps OzHarvest to keep on giving.

Where does the food go, and who gets it? Because OzHarvest depends on what's being donated on any particular day, and it's difficult to estimate or predict how much food may be left over after service or functions, Ronni stresses that the food that's donated is a supplement to the regular meals that often-cash strapped refuges and charities provide. 'We all know how nourishing for the soul good food is - perhaps we even take it for granted - but for the desperate and suffering women, children and older people who don't know where they'll be sleeping that night, something delicious can give them the lift - and nutrition - they need,' says Ronni.

Among the 194 charities in Sydney, nine in Wollongong and twenty-eight in Canberra, these charities include refuges for abused children or victims of domestic violence who have nowhere else to go; single parents with no support; older people who have trouble making ends meet; refugees looking for a better life; the homeless, the vulnerable, the desperate, the poor, the tired, the hungry, the huddled masses we too often step over on the lunchtime rush to the Food Court.

OzHarvest is non-denominational, and the only common feature among these many charities is that they all support the vulnerable, from well-known organisations like Mission Australia, the Salvos, and Youth Off the Streets to many small agencies across Sydney, like the small women's refuge that doesn't advertise so its details don't become widespread; or Our Place, which helps long-term homeless to get the confidence and skills they need to re-enter the workforce. Mollie from Our Place is thankful for OzHarvest: 'When you're juggling big numbers to feed at each meal and money's tight, it's really wonderful to know we can rely on OzHarvest's helping hand.'

But it's one thing to talk about "needy people." What do they say about OzHarvest? Ken, who has slept rough for ten years on Sydney's streets had this to say: 'The past 10 years have been very hard on both mind and body, but one thing has made the past five years bearable and that is OzHarvest. They don't only feed people like me with fresh and nutritious food but they supply drop-in centres right across Sydney. We, the homeless, are forever grateful for the caring people of OzHarvest. We love and thank you OzHarvest.'

OzHarvest's Recipe for Feeding People

The most important thing you need to know about this recipe is that there aren't any secrets methods, hard to find ingredients or complicated cooking techniques. It's all achievable by anyone and best of all, there aren't any calories to count and most of the time there isn't any cleaning up to do at the end either.

ingredients
1 telephone or computer with internet access
1 handful of restaurant, catering company or other successful hospitality business
Bunches of delicious and fresh food that would otherwise be thrown out

method
Contact OzHarvest on 02 9516 3877 or at info@ozharvest.org

Let your friendly operator know what type and quantity of food you'd like to donate.

Depending on where you are in Sydney, Canberra or Wollongong, OzHarvest can collect from you between once and six times a week - Sunday collections must be specially arranged. Arrange a time and place for pickup.

Make sure all perishable food's refrigerated until your preferred designated pickup time. Only donate chilled, frozen or dry food - don't donate hot food unless it's been chilled down first and hasn't already been reheated. Chill hot foods down from 60°C to 21°C within the first two hours and to 5°C within the following four hours before OzHarvest collects them.

Make sure all food for collection, including frozen food, is not less than 48 hours to its use-by or expiry date. OzHarvest will accept products that display their best-by dates but these must be in good, edible condition.

Make sure you package the food securely so it can be safely transported - you can use sealed containers, takeaway containers or insulated packaging, but if you don't have any ready, let OzHarvest know and they'll provide you with packaging.

Let your staff know you're expecting OzHarvest so they're ready to know what to do when OzHarvest arrives (see the Things to Remember below).

Include a brief description of the food you're donating, including any allergens it might contain, such as nuts, dairy, soy, egg or gluten. Include any instructions you may wish to add to assist customers to reheat, reuse and enjoy it.

Just wait for us to come pick everything up and make sure to stay in touch in case anything happens or comes up!

Things to Remember when You Donate to OzHarvest:
OzHarvest cannot accept cooked rice, or any kind of shellfish.

Because of some of their clients' needs and profiles, OzHarvest cannot accept any food with any alcohol in it, like Coq au Vin, Beef Burgundy, Brandy Sauce, Beer-Battered anything, or any other marinades or sauces that may contain alcohol.

For more information on what you can and cannot donate, and anything else you'd like to know, get in touch with OzHarvest, or check out its donation

green tips

Save your waste - and your waist!
Don't just buy smaller amounts regularly to reduce waste. Eat only what you need - don't pile up the plate and throw most of it away. Portion sizes have quadrupled in the last thirty years, resulting in "affluence diseases" like obesity, diabetes and heart disease. So dish up a third of what you'd normally put on the plate - if you want more, have seconds. You'll find you lose weight and reduce waste - as well as having more leftovers to take for lunch and save on takeaways.

Feed someone with a mouse click
You may not be able to volunteer or donate to OzHarvest, but why not do something quick, painless and easy to help alleviate world hunger? Just go to the Hunger Site (www.thehungersite.com) and click on the donation button - every click's sponsored by generous corporations who pay for banner ads on the site, the proceeds from which are used to donate food to the world's hungry via recognised charity partners such as the US Mercy Corps, the Charity Advisory Trust and others. Last year it donated over 65 million cups of food. Make it your homepage, click when you log on, and spread the word - it won't cost you more than a click!

OzHarvest Australia
P O Box 255
Alexandria NSW 2015
Ph: 02 9516 3877
info@ozharvest.org
www.ozharvest.org
With branches in Sydney, Canberra and Wollongong, and plans to open nationwide in line with available

Bird Cow Fish

Alex Herbert

Although she studied history and languages at the University of Sydney, Alex Herbert's first passion was always good food home-cooked and from the heart. Growing up in Sydney's leafy North Shore she loved watching her mum, aunts and grandmother busy and laughing in the kitchen, and so it was inevitable she would end up cooking, taking up an apprenticeship at the famed Berowra Waters Inn, under the tutelage of those doyens of Australian cuisine, Gay Bilson and Janni Kyritsis. Berowra Waters didn't just give her her start in the cooking professionally - it was also where she met the father of her two sons Luke and Joel, Howard Gardner.

After the outstanding success of their first restaurant together, the still-legendary Pine Log Restaurant on the NSW Central Coast, which won the 1993 Sydney Morning Herald Good Food Guide's Country Restaurant of the Year, Alex took up the pans at some of Australia's best restaurants, including Maggie Beer's Pheasant Farm Restaurant in South Australia; Christine Manfield's Paramount Restaurant in Sydney; and David Thompson's Sailors Thai, where she met old friend and long-time collaborator, Longrain's Martin Boetz, who worked with her as co-chef at the original Bird Cow Fish in 1996.

Alex also branched into retail, co-establishing DeLish Store in Lindfield between 1998 and 2002; then went on to build her food consultancy business to clients such as Trippas White Catering at the Art Gallery of NSW; and starting the media career that would see her featured in books by Sophie Zakolar and Maggie Beer and acting as a consultant and mentor to the Network Ten series The Cooks - not to mention her regular appearances on radio and TV!

And in the middle of all this and raising two lovely, lively boys, Alex found the time to re-open Bird Cow Fish in 2006 to her fans' delight, specialising in simple, elegant and harmonious food, using her extensive network of conscientious and committed suppliers to provide the very best ethically, sustainably and locally-produced green food.

You're such a multi-talented person! Do you have any specialties?

You could say I'm a bit of an all-rounder! I've done a lot of different jobs in a wide range of restaurants, from starting in the pastry section at the fine dining Berowra Waters Inn twenty years ago, running the more casual Hardy's Bay RSL bistro, to doing stints at the modern Asian Sailors Thai and Longrain.

What do you like eating?

I like to eat just about everything! I'll try anything once - the most adventurous thing I've probably eaten was bull's testicles, at the Symposium of Gastronomy in Orange NSW. It was part of a feast offered by some wonderful local chefs and it's not something you often get the chance to try, so I just had to do it. If I remember correctly, they were crumbed and fried, a bit like brains - crispy on the outside and not chewy at all. I don't think they were that bad, actually!

How do you keep things fresh and interesting?

I head out to Sydney's Flemington Markets every Thursday morning and just get so inspired by the wonderful produce and the amazing people who grow it and bring it to market. I love food markets for that very reason: meeting the growers and connecting with your food and where it comes from really makes you want to get cooking!

How has home cooking changed in the past twenty years?
It's gotten better *and* worse. It's such a fast-paced world now that lots of us work much longer hours and feel that pressure intrude into our home life. With such little time to enjoy downtime - let alone cooking and eating well - many people have taken shortcuts like eating more processed or packaged foods or takeaways. Food's become more fashionable but it's not necessarily become the integral part of life that it is, that it should be.

But do you think that with food having become more "fashionable," people will become more interested in food, especially green food, and more likely to make better choices?
Unfortunately, in Australia, our population's relatively small. So smaller growers or farmers committed to organic, free-range, sustainable green food don't enjoy the same demand as their counterparts in countries with much bigger populations, like, say, the United States or United Kingdom. This does mean that our green food does cost more than, say, there, or in comparison to conventionally produced, plastic-wrapped supermarket food. But again, although food's become more fashionable, faced with the choice, how many people would be prepared to pay more for lovingly-grown, organic, free-range, sustainable green food, as opposed to paying top dollar for the latest fancy handbag?

If there was one thing you could change about the food you serve, what would it be?
I wish I could charge what it was really worth, so I could pay my staff more. They're vital to our success, because they're the drivers at the steering wheel of Bird Cow Fish. It also affects the menu - I've got to be careful using very expensive ingredients like, say, truffles, because our budget mightn't allow for them, and besides, many diners wouldn't always understand or appreciate their cost.

So, given its higher prices, why have you embraced a green food approach?
Apart from it just being the right thing to do, like many chefs, I believe it just tastes better too. Besides, it's something we, as food professionals, should encourage and promote as we do our bit to educate our customers about the benefits to their health and the environment.

Is it important that it's organic?
I think the philosophies behind organic food are great, and debates about the merits of organic and conventional foods are important mainly because they highlight the need for discussion about where our food's come from, how it's been produced, and how it's been handled. Even if those messages get diluted, at least they hopefully get people asking 'What's in those chicken nuggets?' And it's not pretty!

I do try to use as much organic produce as I can and where the product deserves its premium. For example, I just love Nolan's Road Certified Organic Kabuli Chickpeas in my Roasted Mirrool Creek Lamb Loin with Braised Globe Artichokes, Nolan's Road Organic Chickpeas and Celery. Unfortunately, although I think organic food's wonderful, I just can't afford to only use it all the time, and besides, there are lots of amazing producers doing great things but who just aren't certified.

What about genetically modified food?
We definitely need to know more. Personally, I think GM foods are mostly corporate-driven for short-term profit, with little thought for the future and even less information provided to the consumer. I understand the need to protect intellectual property - if you can apply it to produce - but it seems so secretive, and we need to learn a lot more about GM food and the potential effects and consequences. Of course, everyone has a right to eat whatever they like, but equally, they have a right not to, and especially after making an informed decision.

What challenges does seasonality bring? And what's your favourite season for cooking?
I love the challenges of seasonality. We're always changing our menu, depending on what our suppliers bring us or what we find at the Markets. I've tried to cultivate close relationships with all our suppliers and growers so they can keep us informed about what's good, what's coming up, and making that extra little effort to ensure we can serve our diners with the very best every season has to offer.

Having said that, I love cooking in autumn with wonderful autumnal produce such as celeriac, fennel and artichokes, which are some of my most favourite ingredients.

What ingredients would you encourage others to use?
Anything free-range, organic, ethically and sustainably produced - especially biodynamic, free-range, organic eggs laid by happy, well-cared for chooks! We make a point of supporting and celebrating our suppliers on our website, so everyone can see and know exactly what we serve, where it came from, and who produced it - so hopefully they can support them too.

Any food that's come direct from the farmer is bound to have a provenance and history you can rely on, reflected by their growers' commitment and passion.

What other green food processes have you implemented?
We've sought professional energy and waste saving advice, making sure we reduce waste and packaging, recycling, making sure lights and ovens are only on when needed, using 100% recycled paper for all our menus, and we've just started trialling 100% recycled paper takeaway coffee cups, which is exciting!

Venue

Right in the heart of Surry Hills's funky Crown Street fashion and food precinct, Bird Cow Fish joins a long list of some of Sydney most illustrious foodie Meccas. Catering to a diverse and cosmopolitan local community, Bird Cow Fish has become a part of the area's growing food culture. With a discreet and elegant ambience that reflects Alex and Howard's simple yet sophisticated approach to food, its aged wooden floors and warm subtle lighting welcome everyone, from busy commuters grabbing a morning espresso fix and Belvoir Street Theatre patrons enjoying a pre-show bite; to ladies who lunch and locals enjoying the many pleasures of a lazy weekend brekkie.

Enjoy a heart starting Single Origin espresso or loose leaf tea, Penelope Sach herbal infusion, or, if it's the morning after a big night, Bird Cow Fish's famous and restorative Bloody or Virgin Maries - especially with some of the brunch that brings punters back again and again: the ever-popular Crooked Madame, Alex's twist on the classic French cheese and ham toastie; the rich Three-Egg Omelette with Creamed Celeriac and Watercress on Sonoma sourdough bread; or the indulgent Chocolate Brioche French Toast with Caramelised Banana and Vanilla Custard.

Reflecting Alex and Howard's motto of "good, simple, delicious" fare, enjoy the Espresso Bar's ever-changing share plates, including the fresh Tartare of Ocean Trout and Fresh Herbs with Beetroot Jelly, Horseradish Cream and Crispbreads; the Terrine of the Day with Bitter Leaves and Sourdough Bruschetta; or a selection of Pino Tomini Forest's Cured Meats, Yarra Valley Fetta, Grissini and Vincotto, along with a wide selection of premium Australian and international wines, beers and liqueurs.

For a long lunch or pre-show meal, enjoy the Bistro's regular meal deals with some of Alex's best dishes, including Potato Gnocchi with Prawn Meat Sautéed in Burnt Butter, Verjuice, Capers and Crispy Sage; Roasted Prosciutto-Wrapped Boned and Rolled Chicken with Cauliflower Purée, Shiitake Mushrooms and Porcini Butter Sauce; or the divine Sardine Tartine, Crumbed Sardine Fillets with Tomato, Cucumber, Red Onion, Mint, Basil, a Soft Egg and Bruschetta.

Food and Ingredients

Alex humbly describes her cooking as 'unpretentious,' but the accolades she's accumulated in her long career reflect how much that honesty and simplicity is loved. Awards include Restaurant and Catering Australia's 2006 New Restaurant of the Year, and a coveted Chef's Hat in the prestigious Sydney Morning Herald Good Guide every year since 2007.

Alex's passion to good, simple, delicious food and commitment to supporting the best local producers and growers is clear from the credit given them on the Bird Cow Fish website and on its menus. Sonoma sourdough breads, Velluti's fruit and veg, Tasmanian Cape Grim pasture-fed beef from Andrews' Meats, Egganic Eggs from Orange.

Alex's celebration of regionality has led to some special events such as Bird Cow Fish's regular Regional Wine and Produce Dinners, showcasing the diversity and bounty of Australia's many great wine regions; and her spectacular Food Writers' Dinners, featuring the food and philosophies of some of the world's best and most-influential chefs and writers, including Alice Waters, Fergus Henderson, Maggie Beer and others are always sell-outs.

In addition to her many different roles as chef, consultant, author, educator and mother, Alex's belief in supporting local growers and love of farmers' markets has led to Bird Cow Fish's regular market stall at Redfern's popular Eveleigh Markets, where in addition to feeding hordes of ravenous shoppers with signature dishes like the Crooked Madame, GRANny's PiaOLA or Banana Bread Starcakes, she provides some of Bird Cow Fish's classic favourites to take away, including home-baked Panforte ('great with coffee, and especially with blue cheeses,' she says); a range of seasonal Bird Cow Fish jams; her famous Bird Cow Fish BBQ Sauce; and Bird Cow Fish Bircher Muesli - as well as a $100 gift voucher to lucky members of the Bird Cow Fish mailing list (you can sign up and check out previous editions at www.birdcowfish.com.au/newsletter.htm).

Mornings at the Eveleigh Markets stall are the thing she looks forward to most, apart from spending time with the boys. 'Once the coffee's been drunk and the blur of the past week's been wiped from my eyes, by 4.15am, when the ovens are hot and the kitchen's buzzing, there's nowhere else I'd rather be.'

Crooked Madame

for one sandwich

An indulgent twist on the classic French ham and cheese toastie, this is one of Bird Cow Fish's most popular snacks, both at the Bistro and Redfern's Eveleigh Markets, where you'll find Alex and the team bright and early every Saturday. For a really Bird Cow Fishy experience, try Alex's famous zingy BBQ Sauce!

ingredients

2 slices sourdough bread, 1.5 cm thick
2 eggs, fried to your liking
80g double ham, thinly sliced or shaved (about 3 slices)
2 slices Heidi Gruyère cheese
1 tablespoon Dijon mustard
Bird Cow Fish BBQ Sauce (or any sauce you like)
butter
sandwich press

method

Butter sourdough, then turn over as these are your outside slices.

Fry eggs to your liking. Reserve

Place ham on unbuttered side of one slice. Smear ham with Dijon mustard and barbecue sauce. Top with fried eggs, Heidi Gruyère cheese and remaining bread.

Toast in hot sandwich press until crisp on outside and warmed through.

green tips

Save waste and recycle
There's no point recycling if you're producing lots of packaging and food waste! Avoid packaged food, especially packaged fruit, vegetables and meat, and make sure you use everything - everything you can't use can go back to the garden via the compost or worm farm, or separate your glass, plastic, aluminium and paper into recycling bins. And don't forget leftovers can make wonderful new dishes, like stale bread for croutons, breadcrumbs, Italian bread soup or Mediterranean bread salad!

All waste isn't just garbage, it's wasted money
You wouldn't throw $100 bills into the garbage, but throwing away the estimated $5.2 billion of food Australians waste every year isn't just doing exactly that, it also adds to the dire state of landfill around the country, filling the ground with rotting food. So, again, use everything, or else recycle it into compost - you'll be amazed at how much you save, and how much waste you reduce!

Look before you eat!
With so much more information and awareness - and especially the internet - there's really no excuse not to do a little research and find out where your food's come from and what's in it. Ask yourself: if you knew exactly how that junk was made, and what it was made with, would you be happy to put it in your mouth - or your kids'? There's a reason an apple a day keeps the doctor away - could you say that about chicken nuggets?

Bird Cow Fish
Shops 4 & 5, 500 Crown Street
Surry Hills NSW 2010
Ph: 02 9380 4090
info@birdcowfish.com.au
www.birdcowfish.com.au

VictorsFood

Victor Pisapia

Seasoned New Yorker Victor Pisapia's long and illustrious hospitality career began with his 'greatest influence: my Italian mamma, and her love for food and giving,' he says. 'I used to deliver homemade pizzas every Friday night to half the town I lived in. No one ever paid because my mother fed everyone out of love.' His love of food was matched by his passion for teaching, and after teaching in the ghetto of Wilmington, Delaware, he realised that 'the strength you needed to do that job everyday was superhuman.'

Out of the frying pan, so to speak, he spent a fruitful year travelling around Europe. Discovering interesting and exciting new foods through sharing the hospitality of the many generous people he met, he realised that food was a wonderful and powerful way of bringing people together. Finding himself in the picturesque Delaware resort town of Rehoboth Beach, he established the popular Back Porch Café, where 'the style and excitement came from my Italian heritage and my European travels,' says Victor. 'Everything was made from scratch, and it's there I learnt "fresh sells."'

From there, he went on to study under some of New York's best culinary teachers at the famed New School, before building an empire of six more award-winning restaurants around the United States, such as The Blue Moon Restaurant in Rehoboth Beach and The Rose Tattoo on Quay West Florida, popular with celebrity regulars like Calvin Klein. 'Hey, it was the Eighties!' he says laughing. 'It was wild, fun and we were doing food people loved. We were like the frontiersmen for New American Cuisine.'

In 1994, Victor came to Australia, establishing the acclaimed Rattlesnake Grill on Sydney's North Shore. He also started developing professionally outside the kitchen. He combined his love of food and teaching, leading to the establishment of VictorsFood, creating memorable, interactive, team-building "food experiences" like cooking classes, corporate events, market tours and even South American culinary adventures. All influenced by Victor's passion for bringing people together with seasonal, sustainably and ethically produced green food.

So what does VictorsFood do, exactly?

VictorsFood is a food experience company, where we conduct corporate cooking classes as a team-building and bonding exercise. The most fantastic thing is giving the tips and confidence to the hundreds of people we meet who often haven't cooked much before. Sometimes, I reckon it's a rock 'n' roll food show, as we're on the road so often! We do food tours to South America, the NSW South Coast and to Sydney's fruit bowl in the far Western Suburbs, taking people on farm tours and meeting local growers and farmers to show them where their food really comes from, and the dedicated people who bring it to market and the table. We do lots of food demonstrations and tastings, and it's great for corporate types, stimulating their creativity, getting them out of their comfort zones, and enjoying the experience of sharing food and green food culture.

Why do you reckon so many high-powered corporate types don't have that basic cooking experience?

I'd say primarily, it's their lack of knowledge - often their equally busy and ambitious parents didn't share the experience of cooking and sharing home-cooked food together. And I'd say it's because of their busy careers - people often don't feel they have the time to cook. But after one of our food experiences, they realise it doesn't take that much time or effort, and I'm very pleased to see that change in them.

Have you ever had a disjointed team or newly-merged business that's come to you in the hope of coming out more bonded?
Well, you wouldn't worry about a team-building or bonding exercise if that wasn't the case, would you? [laughs] That's pretty much what we do most of the time - usually teams of people who don't know each other very well or aren't working well together. I'll meet with the client and we'll go through the issues together and talk about what they want or need to accomplish, beyond the cooking element of the experience. Then I give my wonderful staff those objectives so they're aware of who needs to meet with whom, who needs to work more with whomever. One of our most popular and successful exercises is role-playing the opening of a restaurant - if we can get people talking in an informal and fun way like this, putting aside unfamiliarity or differences to get "the restaurant" opened successfully, and focussing on the task at hand instead of any other issues, we always find they break down those communication barriers and resistances and take that positive energy, communication and cooperation back to the office - on a full tummy!

Have you ever held a VictorsFood experience where the teams have, you know, over-egged the pudding, but still come out with a sense of unity and enjoyment?
Nobody's perfect! [laughs] Sure, we've had the odd bad dish or two - it's only natural with inexperienced cooks - but there's a very qualified chef on-hand to guide them, and most importantly, whip something delicious up for the rest of the meal. It often happens when we let them step out of the box and allow their creative juices to, let's just say, over-run [laughs], but it's the way they work together to save those disasters that's most important. Like all of our clients, every one of our events is different: you've got leaders, followers, people who are very creative and people who just want to slop it on the plate. But it's the process of cooking together that brings them together.

Why do you think people want to know so much about food now, as opposed to say, twenty years ago?
Well, twenty years ago, we didn't really have all this coverage of food in the media - it's everywhere! Twenty years ago, we didn't have the likes of Jamie Oliver or Masterchef educating and inspiring people about food and its preparation, how to cook and eat properly. You just can't ignore it, and a great development is that it's starting to be taught in schools - not just as a kind of bogus home economics class, but an integral part of kids' education.

Do you think within that period that perhaps it was a bit misogynistic the way in which women were expected to tend the kitchen, do you think there is more of a push for men to learn a bit more about cooking now?

It's funny, isn't it? There are definitely far more male chefs in restaurants and commercial kitchens, so it's pretty obvious men love cooking! [laughs] However, I've found that for older generations, at least, a lot of mums and grandmas didn't let their men in the kitchen. It's all changing now. With more women working, I reckon a lot of younger men share the cooking duties, and a lot of younger women tell me that their husbands and partners do all the cooking - and leave the washing up to them! So, given how the media coverage of cooking has grown and changed in the past few years, I think it's inspired a lot of men to take up the pans in a more creative sense. Food's become a lifestyle now, and cooking's an opportunity to enjoy, not just a chore.

What's your opinion on the value of organic food?

I love organic food and personally buy it as much as possible. We always offer an organic option for all our events. From an environmental perspective, it's much better for the environment,

so by making the organic choice, we're doing our bit to save and care for the earth.

From a nutritional perspective, I've done a bit of research and I think the data's still out on its nutritional advantages over conventionally grown food - there doesn't seem to that much of a difference in nutritional value between organic and non-organic produce, but it can't hurt not to have pesticides, hormones and other chemicals in our food, can it? Unfortunately, I think the price difference does make a big difference to a lot of people when they shop, so if organic food wasn't so expensive, I think a lot more people would buy it.

Venue

VictorsFood uses a number of high-tech, state-of-the-art venues around the cosmopolitan Danks Street food precinct in Sydney's up-and-coming Waterloo for their food experiences, with the best cookware, utensils and kitchen appliances to ensure the most enjoyable food experience possible. Importantly, reflecting Victor's commitment to the environment, VictorsFood offers a carbon offset option, allowing clients to offset carbon emissions for a dollar or two per head; and putting his money where his mouth is, Victor also offsets the annual running costs of the business, such lighting, energy and transport. 'We work with Climate Friendly (https://climatefriendly.com/) to ensure we're as carbon-neutral as possible,' says Victor.

'Our credits go towards renewable energy projects to offset our emissions,

and best of all, it's completely tax-deductible, so it makes sense both economically and environmentally!'

For the more adventurous, VictorsFood can take you on exciting, educational and inspiring food tours around Australia and the world. With just a fifty minute drive from Sydney's CBD, you can explore the lush and fertile fruit bowl that provides Australia's largest city with much of its produce. Victor will personally introduce you to some of Sydney's best farmers and growers, and to sample their produce, from luscious figs, organic veggies of every variety, earthy mushrooms - even trying some unusual ingredients like prickly pears and getting to tour a pork and bacon smokehouse, so you can get to know more about just what to buy and exactly what to look for.

There's also regular trips to the NSW South Coast, where you can journey through some of Australia's most picturesque landscape, visiting boutique vineyards, meeting local producers, and enjoying some of the most beautiful bounty Australia has to offer.

And once a year, you can join Victor on a tour of South America, enjoying the exciting, authentic flavours and infectious rhythms of Argentina and Brazil. Cook in the exotic markets of Rio de Janeiro during the day and kick up your heels learning the samba at night; sample the delights of Argentina's famous Cafayate wine region and the majestic splendour of the high Andes!

Food and Ingredients

'I've always believed that food's the best medium for bringing people of all types together,' says Victor. 'For example, we just completed an amazing VictorsFood experience for a large company where everyone usually communicated by email and phone, so nobody got to meet or interact in person with each other very often. So we threw a French-themed event, complete with costumes and French-inspired food. The result was a bond only food could have ever achieved - I'm sure a lot of people will consider their colleagues friends now.'

That sincere belief in food bringing people together is reflected in the popularity and success of VictorsFood's team-building food experiences, and the care and attention to detail that Victor and his team give to each and every food experience, ensuring that every food experience is carefully tailored to the needs, wants, abilities and personalities of each individual taking part. Before every VictorsFood experience, Victor loves to visit his favourite fishmongers, farmers and providores to ensure that every ingredient used is of the highest quality and utmost freshness. Of course, reflecting his commitment to locally, ethically and seasonally sourced produce, and depending on his clients' requests, the menu may change, but that's all part of the challenge - and the important culinary and personal lessons VictorsFood experiences offer.

'We've got a wide range of options, depending on the client's needs, budget or time,' Victor says. 'From the forty-five minute Cook Smart to Eat Well, team-building in a lunchbox; Two Hour Tapas, where we offer different delicious tapas from around the world - at each station; to our most popular food experience, The Ultimate Team-Building Experience. We're always adding and improving - one of our most popular new food experiences is The Masterchef Challenge, with timed pressure tests and a mystery box! All of our recipes are simple to ensure they're easily learned and remembered - and so the ingredients can speak for themselves.'

From food experiences based on organic food or sustainable seafood that engage clients to think about the choices they make while shopping or dining; learning how to make perfectly authentic seafood paella and being seduced by the fragrant aromas of saffron, garlic and chorizo as you make a mouth-watering tapas selection over a glass or three of wine; to tackling restaurant-quality masterpieces like Molasses-Spiced Pomegranate Duck Breast or Whole Peking Duck with Hoisin Baste and Corn Crepes, VictorsFood offers an expansive variety of food experiences personally tailored to every company and individual's needs and abilities. But more than that, as Victor enthusiastically says,

'it brings people together in a shared enjoyment of good green food: the perfect means for better communication and better eating. What better

Devilish Tequila Prawns

serves four as an entrée

This spicy taste sensation is surprisingly easy to throw together and makes for a wonderful, zingy light lunch or entrée. Don't be scared of exotic ingredients like banana leaves, which you can get from Asian supermarkets or the backyard, if you have a tree (just make sure to wash it before cutting and serving). And don't be afraid of flambéing, an exciting and dramatic way of finishing a dish - it's really easy! Add the tequila to the pan, then tilt the pan into the flame to pick it up. As the flame catches, flatten the pan out straight away and shake until the flame disappears, then serve. Visit "How to Flambe" http://bit.ly/prawnflambe

'Like some of Australia's best chefs, including Tetsuya and Neil Perry, I just love Crystal Bay prawns,' says Victor. 'Unlike cheaper imported prawns, they're not grown in sewage, they're not frozen, they're not coloured with additives or hormones and they're the sweetest, most delicious prawns on the market.'

ingredients

12 Crystal Bay prawns, peeled and de-veined
1 jalapeño chilli, finely chopped
2 cloves garlic, diced
1 tablespoon olive oil
1 tablespoon of tequila
1 banana leaf, cut into square
1 lime, cut into wedges
salt

method

Heat oil in a frypan till hot. Add jalapeño and sauté until fragrant, about 30 seconds.

Add prawns and garlic and cook until prawns are pink, about 1 minute per side. Sprinkle with pinch of salt.

Splash pan with tequila and flambé to flavour the prawns. Lay banana leaf on a plate, top with prawns and garnish with lime wedges.

green tips

Choose and Learn
Buy your produce fresh from the source - growers, farmers, providores - get to know your suppliers and learn about where your food comes from and how it's grown

What's in this?
You wouldn't eat a sandwich off the footpath, so why just put anything into your or your family's mouths? If you must buy packaged or processed food, make sure you read the label and you know exactly what's in it - many food additives can be potentially harmful! Yes, they do try to hide the chemicals in food with additive numbers, but now you can buy books like The Chemical Maze (available from http://www.possibility.com.au/) and even smart phone apps to take with you when you shop!

Pass it on
Make sure you teach your kids to become the next green food generation of responsible consumers and passionate eaters and cooks. Involve them in the shopping, cooking and composting, and they'll see how everything is connected, where food comes from, how it's made, and where the waste should go. The sooner you start, the more likely they'll make it a way of life - and hopefully pass it onto their kids!

VictorsFood
P O Box 407
Darlinghurst NSW 1300
Ph: 02 9698 7684
info@victorsfood.com.au
www.victorsfood.com.au

Get the kids in the kitchen and the garden, learning about where food comes from and how it's made. Getting them to help shell peas, mix dough, water the garden or tend the worm farm will keep them busy and introduce them to the joys of cooking and eating. Letting them be a part of the cooking process will not only train them to be independent when they leave home, it'll also make them more likely to understand and appreciate their food - and more likely to finish their dinner, if they helped cook it!

Gastronomy

Miccal Cummins

Miccal Cummins' idyllic Tongan childhood with his missionary parents instilled in him a deep and abiding passion for food. Although qualifying as a sculptor and ceramicist at the Canberra School of Art and starting a successful clothing manufacturing and retailing business, he found his vocation in hospitality, working with some of Australia's best and best-known restaurateurs and caterers, including at the legendary Darley Street Brasserie (the precursor to the phenomenally successful Darley Street Thai) with Leeta Collins and Thai food doyen David Thompson, as well as working in Sydney's iconic Royal Botanic Gardens Restaurant Café and with the prestigious Summit Group with the great, late and much lamented Australian cuisine pioneer, Oliver Shaul. After extensive management, food and wine training, Miccal rose to become General Manager of over 120 staff over four busy and iconic venues, still finding time to further his qualifications and deepen his love of gastronomy with intensive training and extensive travels around Europe.

In 1998, Miccal established what The Australian Financial Review calls "one of the best caterers in Sydney and Melbourne:" the sophisticated, successful, sustainable and much-lauded Gastronomy, allowing him to explore his fascination with diverse, exotic and unusual ingredients and cuisines and his commitment to ecologically, ethically, sustainably sourced and produced green food that doesn't cost the earth.

How did your love affair with food begin?
Growing up in a very large and diverse family, where several different languages were spoken, coming together to feast and share and laugh made food a great middle ground. My Australian grandmother from country Victoria was a wonderful woman and an amazing cook - one of my earliest memories was "helping" her bake bread, although I reckon I was more of a hindrance than a help! [laughs] But I loved being in the kitchen and helping her bake - it was just the most wonderful thing ever, and inspired me to keep cooking and eating.

Did you eat traditional Tongan cuisine? What were some of the delicacies and specialties you remember best?
We did, all on the floor together and with our hands! I loved special occasions, where an enormous feast would be laid out on banana leaves under a long thatched pavilion. It included whole spit roasted pigs and Lu Bulu corned beef baked with coconut cream while wrapped in native spinach leaves; along with sweet potatoes, yams and garden vegetables cooked in an underground oven called an 'Umu. I really loved O'tai, raw fish dish cured with lime juice, coconut and onion and boiled whole mud crabs served from the shell and spread throughout the feast. You could say I got my start in catering helping out at family feasts!

Your team's as diverse as your menu, isn't it?
Well, coming from two cultures (Tongan and Australian) myself, I'm really interested in the way that chefs from different backgrounds and cultures translate those differences into their cooking - sort of like the Nonya cuisine of Malaysia, for example, which draws on Malay and Chinese cuisines to create something totally unique. Everyone in my team's got more than one culture (or children with more than one culture) running through their veins - the chefs range from Reiner Ullrich, a German whose wife is Japanese; to Mario Schwallie, part-Sri Lankan, part-Chinese, married to a Singaporean. My own partner, Wallace, is Hong Kong Chinese, and our executive chef Cyril Miletto's Swiss, so it makes for a real melting pot, for want of a better expression! [laughs]

How does that rich cultural diversity influence your menu?

the last twenty years. And it's been just as deeply driven by the many different ethnicities and communities who've contributed to Australian society and food culture - we enjoy so much more variety of different cuisines, flavours, and ingredients than ever before, and with all those viewpoints and traditions, you've got unlimited directions from which to start creating something uniquely Australian, informed and influenced by all those different ingredients and perspectives.

Do you think the influx and influence of so many cultures which place such importance on food and freshness improved Australian food?
Definitely! That demand and passion - and with many immigrants, particularly Italians and Chinese, who have such respect for good, clean, fresh produce, becoming market gardeners, market stall holders or providores - made many Australian farmers realise that they had to lift their game. And that people were definitely prepared to pay for premium produce.

To keep that balance between your ethics and profits must be a constant battle
Some things are easy, depending on the product. But you still have to be adamant! For example, we converted to 100% free range eggs a long time ago, but the hardest part was convincing our egg supplier that we wanted 100% free range eggs and that we were prepared to pay for them. Often, it's just about doing a little research and hunting down and asking for what you want, like when we found an abattoir in Scone (in NSW's Hunter Valley, about two hours' north of Sydney) that produced the right kind of free range, grass-fed beef we wanted.

It's not always easy being green, but it's definitely worth the effort!

What's your pet hate about the food industry?
It's definitely got to be waste. I hate it, especially the shocking amount of eatable food that's thrown out by homes and especially businesses every single day. So much food's cooked and not eaten -I'm not sure of the domestic statistics exactly, but there's huge amounts of food bought by people that never makes it to the table - it just stays in the pan or rots in the fridge. If you even spent a short time at a supermarket loading dock, you'd see a staggering amount of waste just chucked away. I mean, what do people think happens to all the baked goods and cooked meats or prepared meals that's left over in the food displays at the end of the day? It's just thrown out.

What do you do to minimise that waste?
Well, apart from cutting down on packaging and advising clients on the right amount of food needed per head for their functions, we donate all our leftover edible food to the wonderful people at OzHarvest (www.ozharvest.org), who provide edible meals and food from over 900 other generous and committed restaurants and caterers to Sydney's homeless and needy, and with only six vans, even though they deliver over 6000 meals a day, even they can't keep up with the leftovers we produce alone!

But you've also implemented a green waste reduction and recycling program, haven't you?

Most of our green, biodegradable, organic waste isn't produced at our functions or venues, because everything's been peeled or cooked before they get there. It mostly happens at the kitchen, particularly our main kitchen in Kensington. So we collect it in big buckets at every station and wheel it into the compost bin - we compost about nine tonnes a year. We also changed all our suppliers to sustainable, ethical green food producers, of fruit and vegetables in particular, and even fish, although sometimes it's hard to source sustainably farmed fish. But we're working on that! Even all our cutlery and crockery is biodegradable, made from cornstarch or cardboard.

Apart from the wonderful work OzHarvest does or minimising on packaging and green waste, what other solutions are there to tackling this enormous problem?

Well, the biggest obstacles are our own attitudes - this idea that the "lucky country" is a land of plenty and we can afford to just throw food away is a part of our cultural identity.

If you came from a Third World country, where many people live on less than the dollar a day it costs to donate one meal to OzHarvest, where most children are malnourished or starving, you'd be overwhelmed by how much food is produced and displayed in any suburban shopping centre food court. That sort of visual merchandising, which we in the West have become inured to, is now just engrained. But it's very hard to accept, at least for me, that so much of that food, sitting in hot displays all day, will be thrown out before it's sold.

Venue

One of Australia's most successful catering companies, and one of Sydney's biggest, Gastronomy enjoys the patronage of some of the worlds biggest and best-known corporations, including Apple Computer, SBS Corporation, Lexus and Toyota, Louis Vuitton LVMH, Westpac and ANZ Banks, and the Universities of Sydney and New South Wales; with venues at some of Sydney's best-known and most beautiful landmarks, including The Sydney Royal Botanic Gardens, The Museum of Contemporary Art, The State and Metro Theatres and the Australian Museum, offering a staggering range of menus, function packages and settings, from the grand to more intimate.

But although they've helped throw some of Sydney's biggest and most exclusive parties for corporations and consulates alike, they also cater to smaller and more personal events, including birthdays, cocktail parties, and most fondly, weddings, with hundreds of happy couples praising Miccal and his team's professionalism, politeness and patience as their big day was planned and costed to the very last detail, to ensure that the fantastic food and drink and impeccable service came with the utmost care and the very least hassle.

Every function's important to our clients, and all our clients are important to us,' says Miccal. 'Much of the pleasure that the creative challenge provides comes from the exchange of ideas, imagination and vision between our clients and us - they're the fuel to our creative fire! And the biggest thrill comes from seeing the looks on our clients' faces when they see just how we manage to give them exactly what they wanted, how impressed their guests are, and how happy they are at being able to forget the details and just enjoy themselves.'

That personal care and attention to detail hasn't just brought rave reviews and repeat business from thousands of happy clients, but a trophy cabinet full of awards, including Restaurant and Catering NSW's coveted Boardroom Caterer of the Year an unprecedented six years' running; Wedding Caterer of the Year in 2008 and 2009; Westpac Business Champion of Champions Small Business of the Year, 2003; and reflecting Miccal's deep commitment to green food, the prestigious University of New South Wales' 2008 Environmental Achievement and Leadership Award, which recognises outstanding environmental initiative; and the 2009 MEA Corporate Social Responsibility Award. Such social responsibility includes close working with OzHarvest and Restaurant and Catering Australia's Green Table (www.greentable.com.au), Australia's first environmental education and certification program for Australian hospitality, which supports and recognises green food businesses like Gastronomy who do whatever they can to reduce their environmental impact.

Food and Ingredients

'Everything we do is underpinned by our commitment to reducing waste, minimising environmental harm, supporting sustainable, ethical and local green food producers and suppliers, and celebrating the rich cultural diversity of our team,' says Miccal proudly. These wonderful principles are reflected in Gastronomy's many ever-changing menus, which, Miccal points out, 'are created with seasonality and sustainability in mind.' Wherever possible, all ingredients are sourced in-season, organically and locally; and fair-trade when using imported ingredients, to ensure that farmers are fairly compensated.

This compassion for others' welfare extends to animal welfare, with Gastronomy changing to suppliers who guaranteed that fish, poultry and meat animals were free-range and treated well. Beef's sourced from a bucolic farm where the cattle's allowed to roam free and graze on lush Hunter Valley pasture. All poultry and eggs are free-range and organic. And whatever's leftover is composted or donated to OzHarvest, to feed thousands of hungry Australians.

Whether you're enjoying cocktails and cocktail treats like Mini Double-Baked Gruyère Cheese Soufflés; Little Yorkshire Puddings with Shavings of Mustard-Crusted Roast Beef and Rosemary Gravy; or exciting additional options like a vast Seafood Bar with Whole King Prawns and Market-Fresh Oysters on a Bed of Ice with Banana Leaves, Lime Wedges, Ginger, Soy and Shallot Sauce and Miccal's famous Home-made Cocktail Sauce, you'll know everything is real, natural, sustainable, ethical green food - and whatever you don't eat will go to a good cause.

That's if you can leave anything! Gastronomy's Degustation Menu, featuring some of its "greatest hits" is the ultimate food experience, featuring cocktails like the lush Pomegranate Martini on arrival, with luxurious canapés like Tomato Sorbet with Basil Oil and a Crisp Basil Leaf; and individually-plated courses like Blue-Eye Cod and Celeriac Soup with Saffron and Cinnamon; Chargrilled Quail with Garlic, Lemon Bay Leaf and Olive Oil on a Bed of Rocket; or Moroccan Lamb Tenderloin with Preserved Lemon and Pinenut Couscous, Dressed with Garlic, Lemon Juice and Tahini, reflecting Gastronomy's multicultural menu and Miccal's passion for diversity, which The Sydney Morning Herald's prestigious Good Living praises as "A thrilling combination of textures and flavours, including deft Asian as well as European technique."

Whether it's your birthday, wedding, launch or corporate nosh-up, Miccal and his dedicated Gastronomy team have a range of packages and

Organic Chicken and Tarragon Consommé and Tortellini

for six as an entrée

ingredients

Chicken Consommé - makes 2L
1.6kg free range organic chicken bones, or 2 free range organic chicken frames
2 carrots, halved
3 sticks celery, quartered
1 large white onion, quartered
1 large leek, white part only
1 bunch parsley, stem and leaves intact
3 cloves garlic, bruised with side of knife
1 generous sprig thyme
1 bay leaf
1 tablespoon sea salt flakes
1 teaspoon whole black peppercorns
cheesecloth

Tortellini Filling
150g organic chicken mince or chicken breast, finely chopped
30g ricotta, drained of liquid
1 dessertspoon parmesan, finely grated
15 leaves fresh tarragon, finely chopped
1 eschalot, finely diced
1 egg yolk
half clove garlic, peeled and minced
half bunch tarragon or chervil leaves, picked off stalks, to garnish

Tortellini Dough
250g strong unbleached flour
2 free range egg yolks
2 free range eggs
salt
pasta machine
cookie cutter

method

Chicken Consommé
Throw all ingredients into a large stockpot and cover with cold water. Cover with a lid, then bring to boil on medium-high heat. Reduce heat to medium-low so surface of stock barely shimmers and then simmer uncovered for 3 to 4 hours, skimming surface foam from time to time. Remove chicken, then strain stock 3 times through double cheesecloth-lined sieve. Discard solids, and use straightaway or freeze for future use - it'll keep for up to 3 months!

Tortellini Filling
Mix all ingredients together thoroughly and chill in the fridge while you prepare the dough.

Tortellini Dough
Separate egg yolks. Place flour in food processor or mixing bowl with egg yolks, whole free range egg, pinch of salt and mix thoroughly until you have a fine dough. Remove from food processor or bowl and knead by hand for 5 minutes on floured surface - either kitchen bench or large chopping board.

Roll dough out into long sheets using pasta machine. If you don't have a pasta sheet you can roll the dough out with a rolling pin on a floured bench, but a pasta machine is well worth the investment. With cookie cutter, cut dough into circles - you can either choose to make six large tortellini or 12 smaller ones.

Tortellini
Lay out dough rounds on floured tray and place heaped teaspoon of tortellini filling in centre. Join edges of round together and lightly squeeze edges to make half-circles, then bring corners on long edge around and pinch them together to form a kind of ring of pasta - almost as if they were holding their hands together. Blanch tortellini in boiling salted water for 6 - 8 minutes until they float, then leave for another 2 minutes before refreshing in ice and cold water.

To serve, warm serving plates or bowls in oven at very low temperature for about 10 minutes. Heat consommé in small pot and season with salt and pepper.

Blanch tortellini again in boiling water, drain and place 1 or 2 per plate or bowl. Pour the consommé on top and garnish with a few tarragon or chervil leaves.

Gastronomy,
The Art and Science of Food
P O Box 223
Kensington NSW 1465
Ph: 02 9663 4840
catering@gastronomy.com.au
www.gastronomy.com.au

Selah Restaurant
Sam Pask & Gavin Foster

Despite starting out washing dishes, peeling spuds and boning chooks at the local restaurant in his native New Zealand, Sam Pask's always loved hospitality. And hospitality's loved him back, rewarding him with a long and very successful career all over the world, including working at Peter Gilmore's world-renowned Quay, just across the water.

Coming from a family of butchers and accomplished home cooks, it was inevitable Gavin Foster would become a chef, starting his apprenticeship just out of high school in Perth, Western Australia. His passion and dedication was evident even then, volunteering one day a week for months at the popular Perth eatery Fraser's before landing the job. 'It was there that I learnt about sourcing the best quality produce and cooking it simply and allowing its flavours to shine,' he says fondly.

Moving to Sydney, he worked as a chef at the well-loved Bather's Pavilion on Balmoral Beach, Sydney, before taking up the pans at Selah.

Working closely with Sam, who's proud of his goal of creating a fun, happy, warm and creative work environment, and who shares his deep beliefs in sustainable and ethical green food, Gavin says 'I've found the perfect place to explore my culinary creativity and to live by my personal green food philosophy.' What a recipe for green food success!

How did Selah start?
Sam: After working in some of the world's best restaurants, including a fabulous time at Quay, I was itching to use some of the ideas and experience I'd gained from working in fine dining to start my own - and in 2003, Selah kicked off!

How did you meet?
Sam: After my old chef left, I advertised and up rolled Gavin. We got along really well - I really liked his style and personal manner and we shared the same passions for sophisticated bistro food, lovingly prepared with good green food. We've never looked back!
Gavin: I was attracted to Selah because it was refined and stylish, while still being warm, inviting and intimate. I was particularly drawn to it because of Sam's food-focused philosophy - that the quality of the produce was so important. I'm really grateful that he's given me the opportunity to refine my cooking style while still offering the flexibility to source the best locally-sourced, ethically and sustainably produced green food.

Was green food something you were always passionate about?
Sam: Actually, when we first opened, it wasn't something I'd really thought much about at all. You could say the catalyst for my conversion was my lovely wife Jane. She'd faced some health challenges and inspired her own family to re-examine their own approaches to sustainability - like removing twelve herbicides and pesticides from their North Queensland banana plantation, changing their diet and reading the labels on packaged food, which fuelled their passion for healthy eating and green food. Seeing, from her perspective and example, how much food's poorly or unethically or unsustainably produced and how much carbon and chemicals go into mass-produced food, didn't just make me appreciate the environmental benefits in going greener - the proof was in the tasting! It just tastes so much more delicious, as well as being much better for you.

Gavin: Ever since I was very young, I'd always known that we had to respect the earth, to keep its natural balance, and to try to minimise our negative impact on the environment. That became even more important after the birth of my children: I realised I had to live less selfishly, not just for their sake, but for their future's sake. I really started thinking more and more about trying to be a better, more conscious person, and out of that, a better, more conscious chef. After doing some research and reading, I realised it didn't take a lot to make small but important changes: reducing food miles, carbon emissions or trying to source ethically and sustainably produced green food wasn't that hard, and it made perfect sense. And I was really lucky to find a place like Selah that shared that philosophy.

So what changes did you make?
Sam: Heaps! From sourcing the best, chemical and hormone-free produce, locally, ethically and sustainably grown produce, to reducing our energy consumption and emissions, to the way we cook - if you check out our website, you'll see what steps we've taken, such as not using aluminium cookware because being such a conductive element, aluminium will eventually make it from the pot into your food, and it's been suggested that it can contribute to Alzheimer's disease - I can't remember the exact study [laughs], but why not err on the side of caution? Not everyone who dines with us will be coming just because of the environmental or health benefits, but they'll all taste and see the immense difference in quality.

You don't seem to push the green food factor...
Sam: No, it's not the vibe we're going for. We want you to enjoy yourself, not suffer a sermon! Our approach is more one of integration, infusing our menu and service with our personal philosophies towards sustainability and ethicality. In the past, as we established the business, it was a question of the bottom line, having to pay the bills and keep going; but now we've reached a point where we can afford to implement these small but important changes. We have discussed making more of a point about new initiatives in the future, but only to educate our customers, not lecture them.

There's a great deal of information on your website about the green food you use, the producers who supply it, and your green food philosophy. Is it important for people to have that information?
Gavin: Yes! An informed patron's a very appreciative one!

I think that as people become better informed about what the environment and what they eat, they do want to know about where their food is coming from and the care with which it's grown.

With that education and more coverage of the issues, do you think there's more green food on offer?
Sam: Well, as more consumers become more discerning about what they eat - not just in terms of taste or health but ethics and environment as well - increased knowledge and demand has shown more and more producers that they can provide great green food products. There's been more and more choice available, which can only grow as demand grows. For example, you never used to be able to get great organic Australian olives or olive oil - now we produce some of the best in the world.

Does it take much effort to source your produce? And how does this affect your menu?
Sam: We're lucky that in Sydney, there are so many great suppliers who'll drop the ingredients off at your door. Of course, you do still need to do a bit of "hunting and gathering." It took us ages to find exactly the right Australian mineral water - not just the right taste or price, but ensuring it fulfilled the green food goals we have. But it was definitely worth it! I'm always looking for something new and unique to share with our patrons - right now, I'm trying to find the best micro- or craft-brewery beers - and there are heaps out there made by talented Australian brewers who are as passionate about their product as they are about the environment!
Gavin: It always starts with the ingredient. Trying to be as seasonal as possible, I always look at what the best in-season ingredients are about, and then using both classic and contemporary techniques - as well as a bit of intuition and creativity - I try and create a menu that's in harmony with the season.

I always try to use Australian and local ingredients,

and we always use some of Australia's best-known and most reputable suppliers for organic, free-range and sustainably grown meat, poultry and fish. For example, when considering fish, I always source sustainably wild-caught varieties like … that are low in heavy metals, and when using farmed fish, I always source ethically-grown, organic land-farmed fish with slightly longer growth times - both of which naturally result in a much healthier and much tastier dish.

Venue

Selah's long been praised for its warm, intimate vibe, a welcoming alternative to other stuffy power-lunch places around the Quay. The Selah floor team seems more like a family, headed by the wonderful Mary-Anne Edwards, who enthusiastically proclaims how much she loves all her clientele, and her staff - many of whom have been there for years.

We've got loads of regulars - from business people to Opera House theatre goers, as well as countless overseas visitors. But the buzz is definitely kept going by Mary-Anne and her team.

'Although the bistro setting is informal and unpretentious, the quality of its menu and service reflect Sam and Gavin's passion for good green food and wine. 'The menu's always changing in tune with the seasons,' says Sam proudly. 'And we keep our customers informed with a quarterly newsletter that keeps them informed of special events, as well as offering highlights such as one of Gavin's seasonal recipes to try at home, and a focus on some of the wines we keep in our extensive cellar.'

And, as the favourite venue of some of Sydney's best jazz musos, Selah features once a month on Sundays, acclaimed performers such as 'legendary saxophonist Spike Mason, nimble-fingered guitarist Jeremy Sawkins and Mark Lai and his bewitching double-bass,' says Sam.

Food and Ingredients

Although they don't make a big deal about it at the table, Sam and Gavin's "hunting and gathering" have unearthed some exciting green food finds, and they're not afraid to let you know all about it and its passionate producers on their website, including Blackmore's Wagyu beef, Woodside cheeses, Nicholson & Saville olive oils, Murray River Basin salt, Nice Creams ice cream, Karmee coffee - all painstakingly researched and tasted by Sam and Gavin to ensure they are produced as good as they taste!

You can see that passion and quality in Gavin's famous Byron Bay Black Berkshire Pork Belly, made with the finest organic, free-range Black Berkshire pigs, roaming on lush Byron Bay hinterland pasture, as well as sweet potatoes, molasses and nuts to further enrich the sweetness and tenderness of deeply marbled and moist pork. Served as an entrée with fennel purée, roast baby eschallots, watercress and a balsamic reduction, it really celebrates the best of the green food generation.

Other featured dishes include Steamed Snapper in Garam Masala and Coconut Curry, Coriander Noodles, Asian Salad and Crisp Curry Leaf, the curry leaves lending this light, fragrant and spicy delight an authentic crunch; or Braised Lamb Neck with Pearl Barley, Thyme and Root Vegetable Cassoulet, Parsnip Purée and Crisps, a classic melt-in-your-mouth slow-cooked braise that shines in concert with velvety parsnip purée and a hearty cassoulet. 'Go on,' says Gavin, temptingly. 'Just stop at one parsnip crisp. I dare you!'

'By using better ingredients, and allowing them to speak for themselves, you naturally create a better dish,' says Gavin.

Sam agrees: 'Sure, the margins aren't as great as if you were only going by price, and you mightn't always make quite as much per dish, but we know how much our guests enjoy their meals - and they usually always bring along a friend next time they dine!'

Olive Oil Poached Atlantic Salmon with Shaved Fennel, Shiso and Sevillano Olive Salad with Candied Orange and Confit Tomato Dressing

serves four as a main

ingredients

Candied Orange
1 orange, zest peeled and julienned
150ml water
100g caster sugar

Confit Tomato Dressing
350ml extra virgin olive oil
6 roma tomatoes
6 sprigs thyme
3 garlic cloves, crushed
¼ bunch of basil, leaves finely sliced
baking paper
foil
cheesecloth

Shaved Fennel, Sevillano Olive and Shiso Salad
1 large fennel bulb
1 bunch chives
24 Sevillano or other green olives
1 punnet baby shiso or other micro herb

Olive Oil Poached Atlantic Salmon
500ml olive oil
4 good sized Atlantic salmon portions, skin on (about 170g each)
4 sprigs thyme
2 bay leaves
Murray River Basin salt flakes

method

Candied Orange
Dissolve sugar in water in a small sauce pan, then bring to a boil. Add zest and simmer gently for 10 - 15 minutes until zest is soft and translucent. Remove from heat and allow to cool in liquid.

Confit Tomato Dressing
Preheat oven to 160°C. Cut tomatoes lengthways and remove seeds. Place tomatoes cut side down in a tight fitting tray, with thyme sprigs and crushed garlic. Glug on enough oil to just cover tomatoes. Cover tray with baking paper and foil. Cook tomatoes for 30 minutes, or until soft to touch.

While tomatoes are cooking, put a strainer over a mixing bowl, then cut a piece of cheesecloth large enough to line strainer and cover tomatoes. Remove tomatoes with slotted spoon, then remove skin and place in cheesecloth-lined strainer - make sure you've got the mixing bowl underneath to catch those drips! Reserve confit oil for dressing. Leave plates or weight in place over tomatoes at least 3 hours, or preferably overnight in fridge. When tomatoes are pressed, remove from cheesecloth, place on a board and finely chop them with a knife. Mix with sliced basil, salt flakes, ground black pepper and enough confit oil to make dressing chunky. Reserve remaining confit oil for later use by storing in an airtight container in the fridge for up to 1 month - it's fantastic as a salad dressing base!

Shaved Fennel, Shiso and Sevillano Olive Salad
Wash fennel, remove stalks and peel off outer layer. Slice very thinly lengthways on a mandolin or with a very sharp knife. Wash and finely snip chives. Mix fennel and chives in a bowl with salt, pepper and a few tablespoons of confit tomato oil, enough to coat thoroughly. Wash and remove stalks from shiso and finely slice lengthways and reserve. Remove cheeks from Sevillano olives by placing olives on stem end and cutting 3 sides off. Reserve

Olive Oil Poached Atlantic Salmon
Buy good Atlantic salmon fillets and ask your fishmonger to bone them for you. Gently heat olive oil in a heavy based saucepan to a constant temperature of 60°C. Place trout gently in oil and poach for 10 - 12 minutes. When cooked, Atlantic salmon should be pink all over, with no white spots - these indicate it's overcooked, so get it out!

To serve place Shaved Fennel Salad in centre of plate then carefully remove Olive Oil Poached Atlantic Salmon from pot with spatula and drain on kitchen paper. Place on top of Shaved Fennel Salad. Spoon Confit Tomato Dressing and scatter Sevillano olive cheeks around plate. Place Candied Orange Zest on top of tomato and olives, then garnish with baby shiso or micro herb sprigs.

Selah Restaurant
12 Loftus Street
Circular Quay
Sydney NSW 2000
Ph: 02 9247 0097
selah@selah.com.au
www.selah.com.au

Courtney's Brasserie
Paul Kuiper

Nothing could keep Paul Kuiper away for long: neither catering 800 meals a day at the Sydney Olympics nor working at Chez Bruce, Pied à Terre and other leading London restaurants. For Paul, affectionately known as "Cheffie," home is where Sydney's geographical heart is: Courtney's Brasserie in Parramatta. This love affair, spanning almost two decades, goes all the way back to Paul's apprenticeship in 1988. He went on to become sous-chef, executive chef and then, finally, the owner of Courtney's, one of Sydney's oldest and best-loved restaurants. After consolidating from 300 covers to an intimate 30, Paul's motto is back to basics with a focus on sustainability; supporting farmers by purchasing directly and as locally as possible; and only using seasonal produce. Every day the menu changes to accommodate the plentiful produce that Paul collects on his way to work - a treat for staff and customers alike!

How would you best describe your cooking style?
Traditional, old-fashioned but wholesome good traditional cooking, influenced by French, Italian and English cuisine. In Bologna, they've perfected the flavour of simple foods over centuries using only local produce. Burgundy's the same, and these flavours are what the rest of the world bases their tastes on.

What types of food do you like to cook?
Everything! The reward's in tasting what you've created from a pile of random ingredients. We might get a box of cauliflowers instead of lettuce, and suddenly we're substituting one dish for another, pickling cauliflowers and making soup, purées and gratin out of them. We've had to change the way we think, but it keeps things fresh and interesting.

So you really are a "back to basics" kind of guy?
Absolutely! I love the simple things that lead the rest of the meal. Like bread: think sandwich, or soup, or braised dish. Or puff pastry that leads to tart, pie, pâté en croute or apple tarte tatin. I love older style cooking. Making terrines, pâtés, braised dishes, offal and pastries.

What foods wouldn't you eat and why?
McDonald's. Ethical and economic reasons aside, it's just not good food. The money would be better spent on a box of vegetables.

If you had your own food show, what would you call it, and why?
I'd call it What the Farmer Said because it all comes down to a story. Every ingredient's got a story, and the farmer is the best person to tell it. I deal with fifteen farmers every week, and when I collect food, I hear such amazing stories every day. Stories about the weather and how it affects their crops, stories about how hard they work to raise the food we eat, what they go through to get it to us. If we think chefs work hard, you should look at farmers - they're doing 70 to 80 hours a week!

Describe your last meal on earth. What would it be, and who would you share it with?
A Sunday meal with the family. In winter it'd be a roast, definitely. A pork roast - a leg or shoulder - with crisp crackling and lots of roast vegetables - potatoes, onions, parsnips, sweet potatoes, carrots, pumpkin, and cauliflower in white sauce. And in summer, probably a barbecue. On the barbeque would be good sausages and rissoles, sirloin steaks and marinated chicken. I'd wash it down with a good Margaret River cab sav.

Why have you embraced a sustainable/local/free-range approach to your food?
Besides the fact that the produce is better, fresher and more rewarding, I was trying to find a way of simplifying the style of food we did at Courtney's. This started with the idea to buy direct from farmers, which meant buying locally. When I started to look, there was so much available in the Sydney basin that I was able to support the farmers by passing on the money to them directly, and not third-hand with commissions. Sustainability is important to me and I get great enjoyment from taking my kids to suppliers' farms, or just growing things at home. Teaching them about the cycle of planting, harvesting and giving back to the ground with composting.

How important is organic food to you?
I think it's very important in the cycle of nature. We need to put back what we take out of the soil in nutrients - we can't just go on stripping the soil and adding chemicals. We shouldn't take short cuts. It's possible to grow almost anything doing it the natural way, and it uses less water. Farmers need to care for the land and nurture it. I know one beef grower who puts all the scraps and bones from the abattoir into his compost to return it to the soil. We get better-tasting produce by growing food the natural way.

What makes your restaurant unique?
Hand-selected produce that's sourced directly from local suppliers. People love to know where their food comes from and that I personally choose it. We've got a blackboard with a map showing all the locations from where we source our produce, and we name every single farmer who supplies to us. I'm always looking to buy direct from the grower. I also like to display food as it is - natural, from the earth. I brought in some branches from my mandarin tree and put them in the restaurant - branches with the bright mandarins still on them - and I have a display of chestnuts still in their prickly shells, looking very different from the glossy nuts in the supermarkets. It's definitely a talking point. Regulars who've come and seen the change to buying local are thrilled, and always comment on how different the food is, all the freshness and flavours.

So, aside from feeding your customers, you think that restaurants have a responsibility to actually educate them on food?
Yes, I do, and I worry that there aren't enough that do do that. I think the more you tell a customer, the better it is for your business.

What influence do you have on the selection of produce you use?
Once I started approaching the farmers, and explained what I wanted to do, they were all pretty keen. It probably took about three months to get it off the ground, but in the last eighteen months, it's grown from just a few suppliers, to being able to source almost everything. Now I can get flowers from the Oakdale Valley; rabbit, venison, or wild deer from Mudgee; organic lamb and beef from Marion Plains; and cheeses from all over, from the Hunter Valley down to the Southern Highlands.

Do you hold any special events?
Last October we hosted "Sunday Lunch in the Orchard." We had 110 guests and did a roast in one of our suppliers' orchards, full of peaches, nashis, plums, mulberries, lemons, limes and quinces. Everything we cooked was from local growers. We roasted pork belly, lamb shoulder, beef rump, and for dessert we served cheeses from the Southern Highlands and mini fruit tarts - little apple pies, plum tarts, poached peaches. We were booked out, and people are already asking if we'll do it again. I plan to do it every year. Maybe we'll do it in a winery next time.

If you could swap jobs for one week, what would you do and whose job would you take?
Lance Armstrong, the one-week challenge of riding through the Alps! I like the mental test of running and triathlons. I'm not very good at sitting still.

What's your pet hate about the food industry?
The attitude of a place that forgets that the customer is a guest that you've invited.

Venue

Parramatta is Australia's second-oldest settlement and the home of New South Wales's early governors. The bustling modern city has retained some of its former colonial glory and Courtney's Brasserie is housed in a lovely old sandstone brick building dating from the 1840s, in the Parramatta's historic Phillip Street. It's actually two cottages, side by side, with the 30-seat restaurant and kitchen in one and a splendid function room in the other. An adjoining courtyard, where Paul grows fresh herbs for the kitchen, provides a sunny space for an alfresco lunch, or a quiet evening lingering over dinner and a drink.

From Courtney's founders, Kim & Joanne Torta, Paul inherited the dream of creating Parramatta's most prestigious restaurant. He achieved this by moving into the warmth and elegance of the colonial cottages.

Matching the cosiness of the old brickwork and the burnished wood, Paul and his wonderful staff have a warm welcome for everyone, whether a regular or a first-timer, offering an unforgettable dining experience.

The emphasis is on freshness, seasonality and sustainability with the best ingredients that the best local farms, orchards and wineries have to offer.

The result, a fusion of French, Italian and English traditions with Australian sensibilities, is a menu of confident and big-hearted dishes.
It's real food, with nothing added but the freshest local ingredients, prepared with supreme skill and loving care.

The private function room is the perfect setting for wedding receptions, birthdays, business meetings, convention breakfasts and lunches - all provided with the same warm service and emphasis on freshness. Courtney's also offers a corporate catering service and specialises in boardroom functions, dinner parties, buffets, finger food and cocktails parties for any event you can think of! Naturally, everything is created around the best regional produce, and always in demand, so book ahead to avoid disappointment.

Food and Ingredients

Paul's enthusiasm for only the best, freshest and locally grown produce means that all Courtney's ingredients are sourced within a maximum radius of 200 kilometres from the kitchen. On the way to work, he'll pick up fruit and vegetables from any one of his regular suppliers, buying whatever is in season or recommended by the farmer. Fruit from orchards in Southwest Sydney and the Southern Highlands, olives and olive oil, figs and olive blossom honey from a beautiful little farm at Silverdale.

"Despite Parramatta being the geographical centre of Sydney, there are farms that are very close," Paul says.

"Just twenty kilometres out of the city centre and you're into farmland, walking through a field, picking up veggies or some things like that, straight out of the ground..."

He believes that food grown sustainably is superior in flavour, texture and nutritional value than the heavily treated and fertilized food produced for supermarkets.

"Why is the produce better?" he asks. "Well, most people would know free-range eggs or chooks best, and how much better they taste. Same goes for lamb, pork, anything. I think produce from a place that cares shows that difference."

The food at Courtney's Brasserie makes the most of this fresh bounty, creating simple, traditional and tasty dishes such as Rabbit Terrines with Wild Rabbits, pork, chestnuts, brandy and port; Beef Bourguignon based on an old French recipe, rich with earthy root vegetables and red wine; Pot-Roasted Chicken with Autumn Vegetables and Tarragon Sauce; or Goat's Cheese and Balsamic Beetroot Tart, starring oven-roasted beetroot wedges drizzled with honey and balsamic vinegar. And for the perfect winter dessert, what could beat Paul's Luscious Sticky Orange Pudding? Perhaps only his Rhubarb Shortcake topped with a dollop of thick cream! When there's a glut of a particular fruit or vegetable, Paul and his team make sure nothing is wasted, turning that surplus into pickles, chutneys, jams and purées, which add a sparkle to other dishes.

Although the daily menu changes depending on what new bounty the season will bring, Courtney's also offers set menus, including a decadent seven course degustation menu with appropriately matched wines, offering such delights as Organic Lamb Brains in Parmesan Batter with Mashed Potato and Port Jus; Roasted Duck Breast with Cauliflower Purée; Confit Field Mushroom and Caramelised Onion Tart; or King Prawn Soufflé with Confit Cherry Tomatoes and Bisque Sauce.

More than anything, Courtney's showcase degustation menu proves that being green can be a magical dining experience.

Courtney's Beef Bourguignon

serves six

This traditional French recipe was once on every Seventies dining party table. Basically, it's an up-market beef stew, in which good red wine and slow cooking transform a cheapish cut of beef into a hearty winter dish, guaranteed to satisfy and warm six hungry people.

ingredients

1.5kg beef shin, cut into 3cm cubes
150g pancetta, rind removed and cut into strips
1 bottle (750ml) good-quality red wine, either pinot noir or burgundy
1 cup (250ml) warm beef stock
12 eschalots, peeled
3 tablespoons (¼ cup) plain flour
2 tablespoons olive oil
2 cloves garlic, chopped
1 tablespoons unsalted butter
1 onion, chopped
1 carrot, peeled and chopped
1 turnip, chopped
1 parsnip, peeled and chopped
1 celery stick, chopped
1 tablespoon parsley, chopped
1 tablespoon sage, chopped
1 tablespoon marjoram, chopped
1 tablespoon thyme, chopped
1 handful button mushrooms
1 tablespoon salt
½ teaspoon cracked pepper

method

In an ovenproof casserole, sauté speck in olive oil, then reserve. Brown meat in fat, then reserve.

Into pot add garlic, chopped vegetables and half the chopped herbs and seasoning. Lightly sauté until coloured, then return meat to pot. Add flour and stir through to coat ingredients.

Pour over red wine and bring to boil. Add warm stock and eschalots. Cover and place in an oven to cook for 4 hrs at 140°C.

To finish, check meat is tender before adding mushrooms and reserved pancetta. Bring to boil and skim off fat. Stir in remaining chopped herbs just before serving with boiled potatoes or warm crusty bread.

green tips

Don't waste anything
Use everything in the fridge - there's a use for it all. If you buy it, use it - don't waste it. Buy herbs in "living" punnets to prevent buying a bunch and then wasting three quarters of it - you'll always have fresh herbs on tap, almost like a herb garden!

Stay local and down-to-earth
Buy fruit and vegetables that aren't packaged. Instead, cook from scratch to save money and waste. You only need a little extra time, but it's worth it. Buy from locally to support your local economy and to reduce the distance your food travels.

Keep the cycle going
Grow your own vegetables, compost vegetable waste and teach your kids how to garden. There's so much reward in showing them the cycle - grow it, pick it, cook it, and compost it back to the garden - it's exciting and fun!

Courtney's Brasserie
70 Phillip Street
Parramatta NSW 2150
Ph: 02 9635 3288
paul@courtneysbrasserie.com.au
www.courtneysbrasserie.com.au

Hungry Duck

David Campbell

'I've always wanted to be a chef,' says David Campbell in the quaint kitchen garden that supplies most of his popular Modern Asian-Australian eatery Hungry Duck, in the charming little NSW South Coast village of Berry. 'I've never thought of doing anything else. I started out washing dishes in the local seafood restaurant, Marina's Cove in my hometown of Cronulla. I washed dishes all through Christmas on the promise of an apprenticeship, and when that fell through, I went and worked for their opposition!' he laughs.

Marina's Cove's loss was international cuisine's gain. Completing an apprenticeship with the original master of Modern Asian-Australian cuisine, celebrated celebrity chef Neil Perry of Sydney's world-famous Rockpool Restaurant, he moved to Lord Howe Island on the Great Barrier Reef to become the island's sous-chef. A persuasive customer poached him to manage the upgrade of his hotel group, after which he went on to start a number of high-profile projects around the world, including Los Angeles' chic Millennium Biltmore Hotel, Kylie Kwong's acclaimed Billy Kwong's in Sydney's Surry Hills, and the London branch of that other great genius of Modern Asian-Australian cuisine, Tetsuya Wakuda.

Coming home in 2004, he and his partner Nicole established The Book Kitchen, a groovy café-cum-cookbook shop in Sydney's hip Surry Hills, before making the tree change to Berry, living his green dream of raising and growing his own produce in his own kitchen garden and farm; cooking seasonally, locally and greenly; creating some of Australia's most inventive and intriguing Modern Asian-Australian delicacies; and even occasionally fitting in a surf when his ever-popular restaurant allows!

After travelling so widely, what made you come back to Australia?

Well, with all the wonderful experience we got from working with some of the world's best chefs in some of the world's most exciting places, we wanted to start our own place. So, after an eighteen month search, in 2004, we finally found the place that would become The Book Kitchen. Bringing together our three loves - books, coffee and food - even we were surprised by how well it took off! We were even named as one of the "Top Ten Places to Eat in the World" by the influential critic Irene Verbene of The Los Angeles Times.

Why did you trade such a successful place for Berry?

We weren't actually looking to give up The Book Kitchen. We just wanted to have a country restaurant to complement the city place. Hungry Duck did really well from day one, and I love being here a lot more. I'm close to the produce I like to use, we can watch things grow, and we've become part of a wonderful community. So when we got an offer on The Book Kitchen, we accepted, and we haven't looked back.

How do you find Berry compares to the city?

We actually attract a lot of clientele from Sydney, and a lot of our locals have, like us, moved down from Sydney too. When we first opened, some of the locals thought we were just the new Chinese restaurant, you could say we didn't get quite the response we were hoping for! [laughs] But once word got out, we soon built up a loyal and enthusiastic fan base who appreciated the time and effort we put into researching and preparing our menu. And we actually find that people now prefer to just come to us, rather than making the trip to Sydney - people even drive down from Sydney and Canberra just for dinner!

How would you describe Hungry Duck?
It's Modern Asian in a country setting, with a relaxed and comfortable vibe.

And what makes Hungry Duck so different?
I think all the things I learnt opening my own business gave me a different and deeper appreciation for produce. We had to cut costs as much as possible in the early days of The Book Kitchen without compromising our principles about ethicality, sustainability and quality. For example, we used cheaper cuts of meat, but from the best animals, resulting in beautiful slow-cooked meals people loved. We used cheaper breeds of fish, but always got the freshest and most sustainable. If you look at the classic repertoire of any cuisine, it's usually the peasant food, the simple and neglected ingredients and methods with nothing wasted, that make for the best recipes, and that helped develop the unique cooking style I have, which has been translated into Hungry Duck's modern Asian menu.

How has food culture, particularly green food culture changed in Australia?
Australia's blessed with diverse agriculture, from tropical produce to cool climate wines. We're not limited by an ageing agricultural culture like much of the rest of the world. If something isn't working, we can change it, and when people have an ethical problem with a farming method, like caged chickens, sows or cattle, or they make conscious choices about organic or sustainable practices, the faming community is generally pretty quick to adapt.

How do you feel about organic food?
I think it's important to give back to the earth what you take from it,
and I'm a big fan of green food practices like perma-culture and bio-dynamics, which are different to organics because organic is now become a commercial term which has got residual costs associated with it. I reckon "organic" has just become a trendy word that's made, for instance, supermarket groceries like cookies or organic coffee just way overpriced. Having said that, organic flour in bulk's almost the same price as conventional alternatives.

Do you use local produce?
For us, there's three types of local: within a hundred kilometres of Hungry Duck; grown or sourced in NSW; and grown or made in Australia. Our menu's written daily, depending on what's available to us any given day. We call our local fishermen to see what they've caught; we get our free-range Bundawarrah pork from Temora near Young, which is a five hour drive, but still the closest free-range piggery we could find. We grow a lot of our own herbs and veggies, and we farm and dry age our own beef. We get fresh wasabi from Tasmania, which is the most local we could get in Australia. Unfortunately, there's not any quality soy sauce manufactured in Australia, so we do have to import that, but we do what we can - and if and when a good Aussie equivalent becomes available, we'll use it.

What local produce are you most proud of?

Well, after all the work and love that went into them, our local pasture-fed beef - it's got real, true flavour, rather than just trying to marble with overfeeding and dosing. In our kitchen garden at the back of the restaurant, we grow herbs and veggies, like Japanese tatsoi and shiso, wasabi, chillies and a range of greens including lemon balm and Chinese wombok - to name just a few. Our farm, which we live on only five minutes' from the restaurant, is where we raise and source our own Black Angus beef cattle, Muscovy and Khaki Campbell ducks and eggs. And our wonderful local fishermen, Johnnies Wilson and Blue and their crew bring us their bountiful catch from Greenwell Point, just off Nowra, about half an hour from here. They know just how we like our fish treated and they get it to us within hours of being caught. That'd never happen in Sydney!

But is it economically viable to buy green food for restaurants and homes?

> Hey, if you don't buy locally, then local produce and producers will vanish. And if you don't buy ethically, sustainably and, for want of a better word, greenly, the world will vanish too.

What cost cheap imports? They won't last forever, they're often not sustainably grown - nor is the method they come here - and in the end, prices will rise, with nothing to replace them here. So, the more locally you buy, the more you'll support the industry here, and hopefully more demand will bring prices down. But we're doing alright buying green food here, so it's possible - you just have to make the decision. People appreciate the difference, and they vote with their stomachs - and wallets!

What green elements to do you use at Hungry Duck?

We grow as much of our own produce as we can in our garden, composted with kitchen scraps and food waste. What we can't grow, we source directly from local producers where possible. In the kitchen, we use low water consumption woks, and in the restaurant, we use low energy lighting and rainwater harvesting. And while we try to avoid packaging where we can - which is much easier when you buy local or grow your own - we recycle all our glass, cardboard, aluminium and foam.

Venue

A bucolic little community about two hours' drive south of Sydney in some of the NSW South Coast's most picturesque scenery, Berry's size belies its sophisticated, cosmopolitan character. With antique shops, fashion boutiques, boutique wineries and a burgeoning food culture, it's no wonder Berry's become a favourite weekend getaway for Sydneysiders and Canberrans.

It's no wonder Hungry Duck's become such a favourite since opening in 2008. With a warm, funky and intimate ambience, seating only 45 covers inside and an outdoor courtyard looking out over the lush Cambewarra Ranges, it's a tranquil, beautiful place to enjoy modern Asian gastronomic treasures and the fruits of David's labour, picked fresh from the kitchen garden.

And with all the green food and environmentally friendly measures taken to keep the Duck's webbed feet treading lightly on the earth, it's no wonder Hungry Duck was named in NSW's "Top Ten Green Eateries" in the prestigious 2010 Sydney Morning Herald Good Food Guide. As you'll discover, enjoying its many delights!

Food and Ingredients

Rather than blinding you with science, paralysing you with choice or resorting to using the same sticky sauces over the same variety of ingredients, David's simple and select Asian-inspired menu reflects its constant changes and elegant sophistication. Made for sharing, the menu features innovative interpretations of Asian classics, reflecting the invention and wit of his time at Tetsuya's.

Although it's always changing, depending on the day, the catch and the season, you might find Plantain Chips with Caramelised Nahm Jim chilli sauce, Lime and Coriander make a spicy, crunchy start to intriguing dishes like Crab Ravioli with Seaweed Salad and Soy Vinaigrette or David's signature dish, Sashimi of Kingfish, Lemon, Lime and Fresh Horseradish, bursting with freshness and flavour.

Poultry, raised and pampered by David himself, includes rich and succulent Duck Three Ways, with a Duck Spring Roll with Honey Sesame Sauce and Chilli Ketchup, Rare Caramelised Breast and a Crispy Sichuan Peppered Leg, offering a symphony of textures, tastes and temperate sensations; or Crispy Soy Chicken with Black Vinegar, Shallots and Red Radish, picked fresh from Hungry Duck's garden.

Beautiful, slow-cooked delights include sticky Caramelised Angus Beef Brisket with Organic Oranges, Star Anise and Cassia Bark, just made for Flat Rice Noodles with Organic Egg, Garlic Chives and Cashews; or Caramelised Pork Hock with Green Papaya and Chilli Salad, ideal with Tempura Zucchini Flowers with Ponzu, the heat of the Green Papaya and Chilli Salad the perfect balance to the richness of the Caramelised Pork Hock, and the Ponzu's zestiness tempering the Tempura Zucchini Flowers' crunch. You won't eat fresher or greener Asian Greens with Oyster Sauce or Stir-fried Green Beans with Garlic Chives and Cashews than these, picked fresh that day and all organic, sustainable, in-season, bio-dynamic and local.

An extensive Australian wine list is complimented by a comprehensive sake, shochu and plum wine list, reflecting Hungry Duck's delicious meeting of East and West. Gluten free, peanut free and vegetarian options are also available on request, as are lavish Nine and Five Course Banquets, featuring all of Hungry Duck's "greatest hits" and some surprising new additions. Just make sure you save some space for the refreshing Kaffir and Tahitian Lime Tart, the intriguing Black Pepper Panna Cotta with Strawberries and Plum Wine, or the unforgettable Passionfruit Trifle with Lychee Sake and Passionfruit Caramel.

'Sure,' says David, waving his arm over the tranquil and bountiful kitchen garden, 'it can keep you busy, trying ensure everything's fresh, seasonal, local green food, especially living in a relatively remote place, but it's a big part of why we came down, and why we stayed - that connection with and appreciation of the place you live, the community you're a part of, the food you eat and cook.' Isn't that what life's all about? Good food, good friends - and a clear conscience?

Sashimi of Local Line-Caught Fish with Lemon, Lime and Fresh Horseradish or Wasabi

serves four as an entrée or a snack

A great summery entrée or snack that celebrates Berry's seafood abundance, it can also make for a lovely light lunch.

'I love this dish because it's so simple, so easy and so flexible,' he adds. 'You can use any sustainably caught fish, like sand whiting, snapper, silver bream or kingfish, and you can vary the amounts depending on how hungry you are, or how many extra guests you have!'

For more information on sustainable fish, check out The Australian Marine Conservation Society's Sustainable Seafood Guide, a free summary of which you can download for free at http://www.marineconservation.org.au/WhatWeDo.asp?active_page_id=238. 'Bush lemons are ugly,' laughs David, 'but they taste fantastic! If you can't get bush lemon, an ordinary lemon will do. I get shiso from my garden, but if you haven't planted a herb garden yet, you can get shiso from any good Japanese or Asian grocery or specialty greengrocer or provedore. With a taste somewhere in between basil and fennel, you could also substitute with Thai holy basil - or experiment with whatever takes your fancy!'

ingredients

500g fresh, filleted local line-caught fish, or 1 800g whole fish
1 bush lemon
1 lime
1 shiso leaf
1 pinch pink peppercorns
1 pinch Murray River salt
a drizzle of light olive oil, not too grassy
1 tablespoon of soy or tamari
½ teaspoon of fresh horseradish or wasabi, grated

method

Peel and segment lemon and lime, cutting segments into half. Slice shiso into thin strips, about 4mm wide. Grate wasabi or horseradish and combine desired amount with soy or tamari.

Fillet fish (or get your fishmonger to do this) - freeze the bones to make a delicious fish stock later. Slice fish quickly and arrange on chilled plate.

On each piece of fish place one piece of lemon or lime, along with one peppercorn and a drizzle of oil and soy sauce.

Finish with a pinch of salt and a scattering of shiso.

To eat, roll up a piece of fish around citrus and peppercorn and push it around in a bit of sauce - make sure you eat it straight away or the citrus will cook the fish!

green tips

Eat
You may think you're saving time by buying ready meals or pre-prepared food, but cooking fresh doesn't take that much more time, and if you do a little planning ahead, making simple dishes that showcase the produce, you'll find you're eating fresher, healthier and much better than before! Buy seasonally and you'll always enjoy the best, rather than cheap, hot-housed, inferior imported alternatives. Become more engaged and informed about your food and you'll cook and eat much better.

Pay
Offset your carbon emissions by purchasing tax deductible credits with companies like Greenfleet, which then plant renewable forests. Go to www.greenfleet.com.au for a free calculation of your emissions, and tips on how to reduce them!

Love
Love your life and you'll love your family, friends and food - it's the thing that brings us all together. Eat well and live responsibly. If you love our beautiful planet, you'll want to leave something for all our children, and make the important choices that ensure our beautiful planet isn't devastated by our enjoyment of it.

Hungry Duck
85 Queen Street
Berry NSW 2535
Ph: 02 4464 2323
info@hungryduck.com.au
www.hungryduck.com.au

Bells at Killcare Boutique Hotel Restaurant and Bar

Stefano Manfredi

One of Australia's best-known and best-loved chefs, Stefano Manfredi's had cooking in the blood. 'I come from a family of cooks on my mother's side,' he says. 'My grandmother was an amazing cook, and ran her own restaurant and guest house near Milan. My mother learnt to cook from her, and I learnt to cook from my mother.'

The dishes, memories and way of life connected to fresh, home-grown or locally-sourced produce stayed with him all his life, making him an internationally-celebrated pioneer of Italian cooking. His first restaurant in Sydney's Ultimo, the legendary Restaurant Manfredi, was the only Italian restaurant awarded the maximum three coveted Chef's Hats in the influential Sydney Morning Herald Good Food Guide in 1994. Sydney diners will remember his other successes, including Bel Mondo in The Rocks, which was awarded a prestigious Insegna del Ristorante by the Italian Government in mid 90s - and his weekly column, Seasonal in The Sydney Morning Herald's Spectrum section, where he continues to share his wisdom and ideas with recipes from his childhood and kitchen, using whatever's in season at the time.

In 2007, Stefano took over Bells at Killcare Restaurant and Bar on NSW's beautiful Central Coast for owners Karina and Brian Barry, tending a bountiful Italian kitchen garden which forms the basis for the seasonally-influenced Italian classics he serves to a whole new legion of fans.

What makes Bell's so special?

I'm sure people will come and try it once. But we keep them coming with sparklingly fresh produce handled in a professional and skilfully Italian way. It's simple, nourishing food. But the most attractive element's the whole experience we create here. I think restaurants are site-specific, and we're developing flavours and dishes, as well as an atmosphere and service that's specific to Bells at Killcare.

What are the challenges of cooking in the Italian way, with seasonal ingredients, and reconciling the traditions you learnt from your mother and grandmother with new cooking techniques?

That's always been the challenge for me. Considering new techniques and methods and reconciling them with my roots! I try to present my family's traditional cooking in a modern restaurant situation - which is a challenge anyway, because where we come from in Italy the produce is completely different! Take gnocchi for example, back in Italy they'd use potatoes that were consistently the same. Here in Australia - even the same variety of potatoes might come one week from Tasmania and the next week from Victoria. So the produce is always different! My mother would always make it by eye, judging it by texture and consistency, not following a recipe. And that's what I try to do. I think that's the most valuable lesson I ever learnt from her. To cook by feel, not by a recipe.

How do you translate those traditional Italian approaches to Modern Australian cuisine and conditions?

Ah well, [laughs] "Modern Australian cuisine" - I'm not sure such a thing even exists! If you look at Italian cooking, for example, it's got specific techniques and qualities. Whereas we sort of say something's "Modern Australian cuisine," there aren't really any dishes there that can be specifically associated with Australia or "Modern Australian cuisine." Most have just got a variety of influences from all around the world. In terms of my Italian cuisine, I am informed by Australian conditions and produce, to which I bring my own Italian technique and philosophy.

How important is your relationship with your suppliers, especially in relation to your cooking?
It's the starting point. Choosing the produce is where one begins to cook. Before you even open a restaurant your question is - "what am I going to cook?" And "what I'm going to cook" is going to be wholly influenced by what I'm going to get. There's no way you can make a silk purse from a sow's ear! That's why so many Italians have got little veggie patches in their backyards and grow their own produce. Other Australians are sort of beginning to understand that, and that's why urban Australians are moving towards getting their produce from farmers' markets or growing it at home.

Why now? Why hasn't it been a tradition or way of life as it is in Italy?
Convenience. I don't think there's always been a widespread cooking culture in Australia. When we first arrived in the Sixties, I remember how I appalled I was at how badly my school friends ate! Stinky mutton, overcooked boiled veggies… I was grossed out! But good food and cooking has come with the rise of ethnic cuisines in Australia. Chinese was the first type of food you could get everywhere in Australia - that homogenised, country town RSL Chinese, which always had an "Australian" section on the menu. But the modern embracing of ethnic and fine-dining restaurants really began in the Seventies and just took off in the Eighties.

Do you think these changes in food culture are just a fad?
Well, yes, there's a certain faddishness to it. But once someone's been told to do it by the media and they go to a farmers' marker or ethnic bakery, they realise the beauty in having that connection with where their food's coming from. They also see the difference in the quality! I think there continues to be a disconnect between the farmer and the urban dweller.

Australians have got an almost mythical regard for farmers. I think it's because most of us live in cities.

But at the end of the day I don't care how faddish it is if people are eating better!

Do you think that this new green food culture has influenced businesses to change their ways or other people to change the way they shop?
Yes, but I think it's a slow road. On the whole, people tend to shop on price. We're one of the most world's obese nations - children especially are a worry. As a nation we eat very poorly and don't do enough exercise. It's frightening how popular and successful fast food is in Australia. But fast food has hidden costs to health and environment.

Is there a link between quality, price, and health? Can you be poor and healthy?

I think it's hard to be healthy if your cheapest option is sugary processed fast food. A high meat diet's deceptively easy as it's quicker to cook and relatively inexpensive. But it takes a cultural depth of cooking to make delicious things out of vegetables, grains and pulses. And that's where ethnic cuisine can teach us so much.

You've got a veggie patch and chooks. What's the future got in store?

We've been talking about getting some pigs! But it turns out you need zoning permission for that - apparently anyone anywhere can have chickens, but not pigs. But we're working on that! I'd also like to increase the size of the veggie patch and get a greenhouse. My favourite thing to grow is garlic - home-grown garlic's so different, and it's so easy to grow. I'd love to have it all year round. We compost and feed our chickens with the kitchen scraps. We've also got plans to put together a series of worm farms to break down our compost even quicker.

Venue

Was there ever a more apt name for such a wonderful place to lose your worries and, uh, kill your cares? Killcare's an idyllic place for a luxury boutique hotel, restaurant and bar. About ninety minutes' drive north of Sydney, the coastal village of Killcare's most easily reached by a regular ferry service across the breathtaking Broken Bay from Palm Beach. Located on the unspoiled tip of the Bouddi Peninsula National Park, Bells at Killcare overlooks the area's lush green scenery and perfect beaches.

Renowned hoteliers Karina and Brian Barry bring extensive hospitality and business experience to Bells at Killcare, which they established in 2007. Karina trained at Sydney's Regent Hotel, London's famed Savoy Hotel, and Neil Perry's celebrated Rockpool before purchasing and running The Hunter Resort. Brian came from a wine marketing and public relations background with Brown Brothers, Wyndham Estate and McWilliams before establishing the prestigious Hunter Valley Wine School and co-founding the boutique Bluetongue Brewery. Their unique understanding of regional hospitality has made Bells at Killcare, according to no less than The Australian, 'the closest approximation of a European country house you could expect to find in a coastal Australian setting.'

With horse-riding, deep-sea fishing, kayaking and bush-walking (with maps, guides, tours and even picnics provided on request) to less tiring activities like sunbathing, swimming and a few indulgent hours in the luxurious Day Spa, featuring treatments with the exclusive and uniquely Indigenous Australian LI'TYA products, using only the purest high-quality native ingredients and extracts, Bells at Killcare has something to offer for everyone in its elegant and relaxing atmosphere, with a natural, nautical theme. Amidst Coastal Style accommodation and luxurious Villas and Suites, The Manor House, where Bells at Killcare Restaurant and Bar makes its home, features that expansive, airy verandah where guests flock in warmer weather. Inside, a fireplace keeps it cosy in winter. And for more private or formal occasions, there's also two private dining rooms and a library!

'It's an experience,' says Stefano as breakers crash in the distance. 'When you're eating a steaming piece of beef in red wine with polenta in front of an open fire in the middle of winter, it draws you into a whole experience. That's what a restaurant should do, and we take you to a place that's special. And while in winter it's slow-cooked hearty food by a fire, in summer it's a different experience with everyone in t-shirts coming up from the beach to eat on the verandah, the kids playing outside in the garden. That's what we're trying to do here - reflect the area that we're in.'

That connection to its surroundings and community are reflected in Bells at Killcare Restaurant and Bar hasn't just made it a favourite with the locals - in 2008, it won its first Chef's Hat in The Sydney Morning Herald Good Food Guide, shortlisted as one of three establishments for The Good Food Guide's Regional Restaurant of the Year, and was named Best New Regional Restaurant in NSW by Restaurant and Catering Australia NSW.

Food and Ingredients

Acclaimed at home and abroad and honoured by the Italian Government, the Italian International Culinary Institute for Foreigners and the iconic Silver Spoon, Italy's best-ever selling cookery manual, Stefano says 'if I'm being totally honest, my tastes are simple. These tastes were formed when I was young. They're the dishes my mother prepared for the family, as she in turn had learnt from her mother. They're the aromas and flavours of Lombard cuisine.'

It's these simple, redolent childhood memories, that Stefano says he attempts, through his accomplished and elegant cooking, to 'return, albeit with the very best produce we can grow in this country.' His 'relatively parsimonious' but harmonious childhood was surrounded by industrious self-sufficiency:

'My father's grandparents made or grew everything they needed. My father's brother was a master salumi maker who'd use every last part of the pig to make products that are among the jewels of Italian gastronomy. My other uncle aged Grana Padano and Reggiano cheeses,' he says proudly.

'When I grew up in suburban Sydney, we always had vegetables growing and fruit trees, especially figs, plums and apricots. For me, Bells is a return to those roots.' Apart from tending the bountiful kitchen garden, which features familiar favourites like figs, citrus, herbs and vegetables - as well as some exotic surprises grown nowhere else, like aniseed, chamomile and sculpit, a rare herb with thin delicate, slightly aromatic leaves, prized in Italy for salads or cooked in risotto, soups and even as a flavouring for omelettes and frittatinas - Stefano continues to make salumi with his old friend Pino, reflecting a personality he says has 'rural roots but urban sensibilities.' Still, you may just catch him picking your dinner before donning his apron, just like his beloved mother and grandmother before him!

When he can't grow it himself, Stefano makes efforts to source local, ethical and sustainable green food, such as earthy mushrooms from nearby Woy Woy, oysters from the scenic Hawkesbury River or freshly caught mullaway fish from Patonga. But nearly everything's made in-house, from pasta and bread to gelato, offering every diner an unforgettable culinary journey through the evocative flavours of this great chef's childhood.

Mushroom Frittatina Rolls with Salsa Verde

makes one frittata as an entrée for one, or a canapé for two

'I guess I'm one of the lucky ones when it comes to selecting the best and freshest produce right from the kitchen door,' laughs Stefano. 'Not only are there fresh veggies but as I go foraging, I pick up at least two dozen eggs every day from our free-range, home-reared chooks who live at the bottom of the property here at Bells at Killcare.

'I absolutely love this recipe, because it's simple, tasty and really reminds me of the essence of my grandmother and mother's cooking. Buon appetito!'

ingredients

Salsa Verde (makes 3 cups)
2 bunches parsley leaves
2 hard boiled eggs
2 garlic cloves, peeled
2 tablespoons large capers
6 anchovy fillets
2 slices bread, soaked in milk
juice of 2 lemons
sea salt
freshly ground pepper
extra virgin olive oil

Mushroom Frittatina Rolls
75g Swiss brown mushrooms, thinly sliced
2 free range eggs
1 clove garlic, minced
1 small leek, finely sliced
1 tablespoon flat-leaf parsley, finely chopped
1 tablespoon parmesan cheese, grated
1 tablespoon chives, finely chopped
3 tablespoons extra virgin olive oil
salt
pepper

method

Salsa Verde
Soak bread in milk until moist then, then place in food processor.

Pick and wash parsley leaves. In a food processor add parsley, garlic, capers, anchovy fillets, bread, lemon juice and pepper. Pulse to a rough salsa.

Add hard-boiled eggs and extra virgin olive oil as needed to achieve the correct consistency - it should be textured rather than a smooth purée. Season with salt and pepper to taste.

Mushroom Frittatina Rolls
In a saucepan, heat 2 tablespoons of olive oil and gently fry garlic and leek until soft but not coloured. Add sliced Swiss brown mushrooms and turn up heat.

Keep stirring until mushrooms are cooked through. Add parsley and season with salt and pepper to taste. Place cooked mushrooms in a food processor and pulse 3 - 4 times till chopped but not puréed. Reserve

Beat eggs lightly with grated parmesan and chopped chives and season with salt and pepper. Heat remaining oil in a skillet or frypan until just smoking. Pour beaten egg, cheese and chives mixture into hot skillet or frypan. Spread beaten egg, cheese and chives mixture over the pan quite thinly - because it's so thin, there shouldn't be any need to turn it. It should take 1 minute to cook and still be a little creamy on top.

Transfer to a warm plate, fill with reserved mushroom mixture and roll tightly.

Serve immediately in thick slices with some salad and as much or little Salsa Verde as you like. The Mushroom Frittatina Rolls will keep in the fridge for the next day, and the Salsa Verde in an airtight container in the fridge for up to one week.

Bells at Killcare Boutique Hotel
Restaurant and Bar
107 The Scenic Road
Killcare Beach NSW 2257
Ph: 02 4360 2411
info@bellsatkillcare.com.au
www.bellsatkillcare.com.au

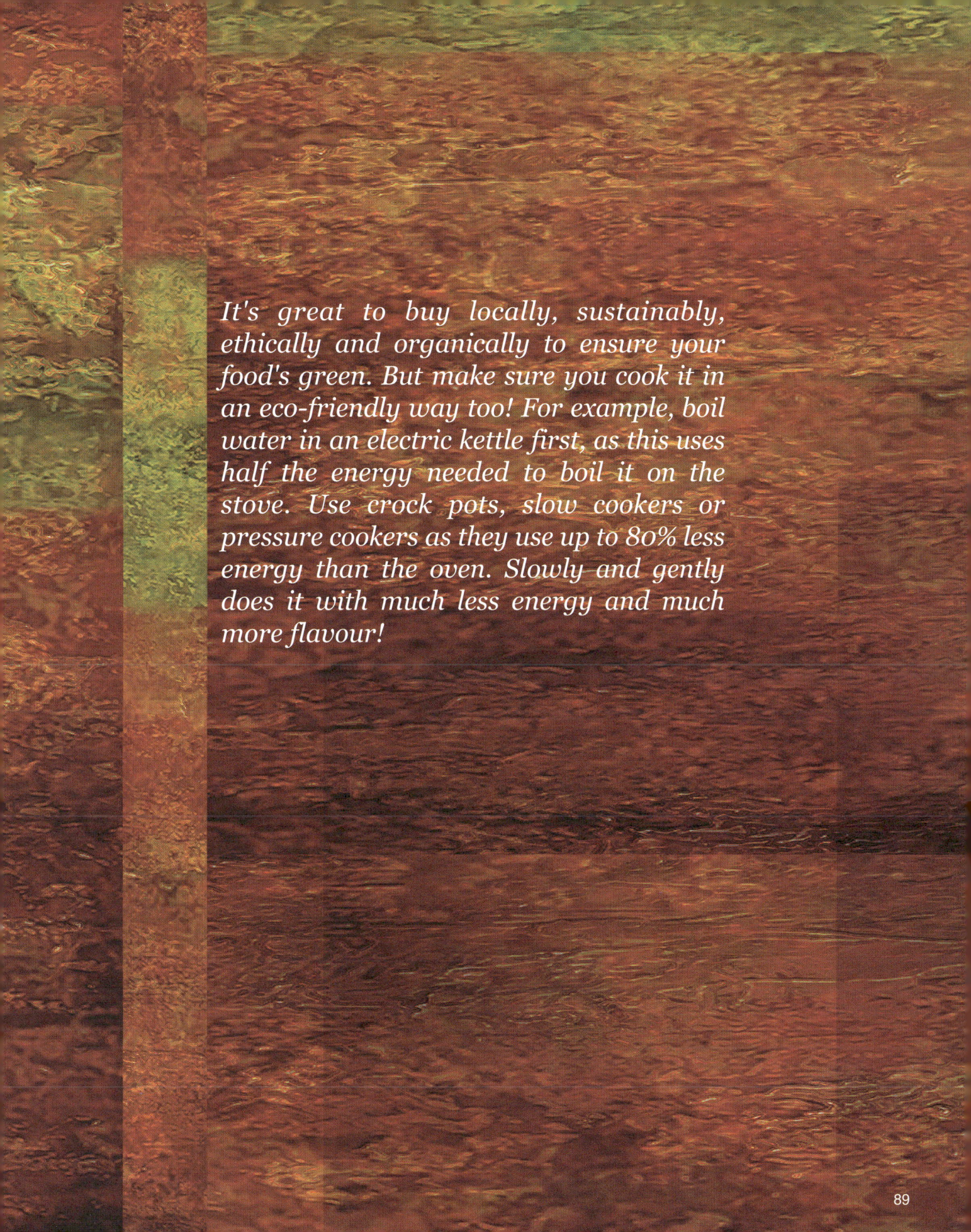

It's great to buy locally, sustainably, ethically and organically to ensure your food's green. But make sure you cook it in an eco-friendly way too! For example, boil water in an electric kettle first, as this uses half the energy needed to boil it on the stove. Use crock pots, slow cookers or pressure cookers as they use up to 80% less energy than the oven. Slowly and gently does it with much less energy and much more flavour!

Margan Family Winegrowers and Restaurant and Tasting Room

Lisa and Andrew Margan

You could say Lisa and Andrew Margan were made for each other. Catching each other's eye at university, they brought to their marriage a Masters in nutrition, specialising in organic food production (Lisa) and two science degrees, specialising in viticulture (Andrew).

After taking Lisa back to the place where his beloved dad Frank established his own vineyard, DeBeyers Wines in nearby Pokolbin, adding twenty vintages under legendary vigneron Murray Tyrell (Andrew), an apprenticeship with renowned chef Robert Molines (Lisa) and throwing in a few fruitful years living and working in France's great Bordeaux wine region, they've come up with a winning recipe for green food and wine success: Margan Restaurant at Margan Family Winegrowers in the beautiful winery village of Broke in NSW's famed Hunter Valley.

After establishing Margan Family Winegrowers in 1997, Lisa and Andrew built an ecologically-sound rammed-earth homestead to house their Restaurant and Cellar Door in 2007, with an adjoining kitchen garden that provides much of the fruit, vegetables and herbs for what's been acclaimed as one of the Hunter Region's best and most exciting new restaurants by no less than Australian Gourmet Traveller, Australian Vogue, the Seven Network's Sydney Weekender and The Sydney Morning Herald's Good Living and Good Food Guide.

'Our motto's "Estate Grown, Estate Made" and we take it very seriously,' says Lisa. 'We want to live off the land and contribute back to the land, which is why we've taken such care to ensure everything is grown and made on the Estate, sourced locally and sustainably, recycled and composted.'

How did you get started as a restaurateur?

Lisa: Having had a background in nutrition, it was an obvious direction, I suppose! I started my apprenticeship under the wonderful Hunter Valley chef, Robert Molines of the renowned Cellar Restaurant (and lately Bistro Molines). Robert's got such an innate respect and feel for food, he really inspired me. This love and respect for good quality produce was deepened when I worked in France for a couple of years, and stood me in good stead when we started our first restaurant, Café Beltree, without any real restaurant management experience - but I've learnt a lot since then, developing the business skills beyond the kitchen to keep paying the bills, running Margan Restaurant as efficiently as possible, and making sure our customers are happy and come back for second helpings!

What food do you like to cook?

Spanish, Italian and French cuisines are comfort food for me - I'm half-Italian so I guess that's to be expected! - but I enjoy discovering the point of difference in cuisines, like Japanese food which employ interesting techniques or unusual ingredients. And I most admire chefs who pay respect to quality ingredients and don't overwork them too much.

What are some of the most adventurous foods you've eaten?

I've eaten some weird and wonderful things! Unidentified protein in Japan and China (the less said, the better); pigs' testicles in Germany; some barely-cooked offal in France - and by mistake, horse meat, which I did not enjoy; and sadly, my aunt Nella's little white

prosciutto and smoked cheese. I mean, it was beautifully cooked and tasted wonderful, but still...

Is there anything you wouldn't eat?
I can't stand over processed foods and prefer to avoid non-sustainable, unethically produced, chemically engineered or treated food.

Are such ethical concerns the reason you've embraced the green food approach to eating and cooking?
I have a Masters in nutrition, specialising in organic food production, and as such, prefer foods to be produced with sustainability in mind. I do have ethical and moral issues with the way a lot of food's produced, particularly the way animals are treated - I try to use free-range meat and poultry where possible so I can enjoy dinner knowing they at least had a happy life before ending up on the plate! But these concerns also extend to the environmental issues as well.

Australia's a fragile ecosystem and farming methods in the past have really not treated the land with respect - you can see this in issues like soil degradation and water salinity. We really do need to take a step back and look after the land, so organic and bio-dynamic production methods really do just make sense.

What importance do food miles factor in when you select your produce?
It's paramount, especially as the cost of freight isn't just economic, but environmental. I'm very hands-on with sourcing and selecting produce and I do try to source as locally as possible. I've got a really big problem with imported bottled water - I refuse to stock it. Having said that, while I try to ensure that most of our produce is sourced locally, the best parmesan only comes from Italy, so I save my food miles up for a few extravagances like that.

More importantly, we've planted a one acre kitchen garden, composted by organic kitchen waste, from which we source most of the fruit, vegetables and herbs in the restaurant's dishes. We recycle used cooking oil into bio-diesel for the farm and winery machinery - and see those chooks? You could say they rule the roost! [laughs] We let them run about, free and happy, fed on our kitchen scraps, and they provide us with the freshest eggs and fertiliser for the kitchen garden. We try our best to tread very lightly.

How would those around you describe you?
Fun. Loyal. Committed. Creative. Hard working. Visionary. Optimist. Happy. Organized. Social. And sometimes a pedantic perfectionist pain in the arse! And no, you can't ask Andrew!

Do you think it is that perfectionism that makes you stand out from the rest?
I'm deeply passionate about good service, good food and good wine. I can't stand mediocrity or laziness when it comes to those, and I won't apologise for being focused on the little details that ensure my customers, whom I wouldn't serve anything I wouldn't serve my family or friends, really enjoy their dining experience with us. Yes, that means we often take a hit to the bottom line to ensure we source only the best, ethically, sustainably and locally produced ingredients, but I couldn't have it any other way. All our suppliers know we expect the very best and if anything's not up to scratch, we send it back - but that doesn't mean we don't nurture close and respectful relationships with them to ensure it always is the very best.

How important are prizes and awards to you?
Hmmm... how do I put this? Very important when you get them, and totally irrelevant when you don't! [laughs] Seriously, though, I view awards and accolades as an opportunity to audit our restaurant - I do try to see it as objectively as a reviewer or customer might, and that perspective helps us keep everything in perspective: especially from our customers' perspective, which is the most important to us. Still, I'm always thrilled to see us collect another award for the mantelpiece!

What would your last meal be?
I'd really love to say a great bottle of Krug Champagne 1996 Vintage and all the fois-gras I could eat - but only because it's my last meal, as fois-gras production often involves practices cruel to the geese like force-feeding, and I wouldn't feel comfortable about it either. Ditto beluga caviar on a warm, crusty baguette with Lescure butter - sturgeon stocks are really threatened so the deliciousness would be outweighed by the guilt. So I guess the one thing I couldn't do without would be the one thing I love eating every day: a bowl of my homemade muesli with soy milk. Oh, and a great chunk of dark Belgian chocolate and Andrew's beautiful wine, made with such love!

A bowl of muesli for your last meal - that's dedication to your beliefs!
Well, it's pretty damn good muesli... [laughs] And don't forget the chocolate!

Venue

A hundred and sixty kilometres from Sydney, the rural idyll of Broke in the famous Hunter Valley may seem a quiet enough corner of the world, but it's got more than its fair share of culinary buzz, with The Sydney Morning Herald glowingly reporting that its "excellent dining is as attractive as the area's renowned wineries." Established as a viniculture centre way back in the 1830s, this beautifully preserved village now boasts over thirty-six boutique vineyards, including Andrew and Lisa's award-winning family winery, Margan Family Winegrowers.

Andrew, Lisa, their family and staff have worked hard to create the perfect place to complement the picturesque surroundings and their dedication to sustainable, ethical green living. Margan Restaurant is a welcoming, rammed earth homestead specially designed by Lisa and Andrew to the highest ecological and energy-saving standards. Inside, rustic floors, high ceilings and an open plan kitchen offer a warm, welcoming and sophisticated dining experience.

From Lisa and wonderful maitre d' Dee-Ann Heath's warm welcome to award-winning chef Ian Atkinson's exciting dishes, including his popular Suckling Pig with Fennel

White Anchovy and Pedro Ximenez Dressing, it'd be easy, as you relax on the expansive deck, enjoying charming vistas of the Estate's vineyards, and in the distance, the stunning Brokenback Mountains - and a glass or two of Margan Family Winegrowers wonderful wines, right from the Cellar Door - to imagine you'd found yourself in paradise. The Margans, their many happy regulars and their very happy chooks would certainly agree.

Food and Ingredients

Given Lisa's perfectionism and expertise in organic food production,

you can eat, drink and be merry, knowing that everything - especially picked from the bountiful kitchen garden - is organic, ethical, chemical and pesticide free green food.

'Whatever we can't grow ourselves,' says Lisa, 'we aim to source as locally as possible to support our community and to reduce food miles.'

And echoing their partnership in life, Lisa's seasonally inspired menu compliments Andrew's award-winning wines perfectly, following their philosophy to keep things minimalist, and to "allow each wine and ingredient to speak for itself."

'I love simple, beautiful food with clean flavours, a balanced palate and carefully layered textures,' says Lisa. 'A bit like wine, I guess!' adds Andrew. Every dish is accompanied by Andrew's thoughtful, sophisticated wine matches, which won his creative and extensive wine list Australian Gourmet Traveller's coveted Two Glasses. Share generous tasting plates, like Roasted Hunter Beef with Pumpkin, Spiced Eggplant, Marinated Feta and Pork Crumbs, just made for the abundantly rich and earthy Margan 2007 Shiraz; or Crispy Soft Shell Crab with Fennel, Lemon Gel and Saffron Aïoli with a perfectly matched glass of Margan 2009 Verdelho.

Salads like cucumber and beetroot, picked fresh from the kitchen garden and tossed with homegrown mint, almost leap off the plate with flavour and enthusiasm; and everyone loves Lisa's signature dish, Linguine with Fried Field Mushrooms, Creamy Organic Poached Egg and Parmesan - an egg even fresher and more delicious coming from the chic chooks who rule the groovy roost outside! Rich and warming Osso Bucco or divine Duck Risotto make wonderful partners for some of Andrew's favourite Margan Family Winegrowers' classic Hunter wines like the 2007 White Label Aged Release Shiraz, its rich ripe berry palate bearing the terroir of the Fordwich Sill of their Timbervines Vineyard, the Vineyard 2009 Range Semillon, with its intense citrus nose, generous middle palate and long crisp finish ideal for those long, lazy Hunter Valley lunches… Just make sure you save room for some of Ian's unforgettable Passionfruit Delicious Pudding with White Chocolate Gelato, or her ever popular Yogurt and Honey Panna Cotta with Fig and Pistachio!

Everything's made from scratch, ensuring it's fresh, unprocessed and lovingly prepared, and the menu changed constantly, in tune with the seasons and availability, and reflecting the Margans' dedication to green food and ethical, sustainable living. The complimentary drinking water's filtered rainwater; the potatoes, beans, herbs and other delicacies picked fresh from the kitchen garden; and anything they can't grow themselves is sourced as locally, ethically and sustainably as possible.

Seared Pepper-Crusted Kingfish and Crispy Silverbeet with Anchovy Mayonnaise

serves four as an entrée

ingredients

Seared Pepper-Crusted Kingfish
4 kingfish fillets (about 80g each)
sea salt flakes
cracked black pepper

Crispy Silverbeet and Leek
3 leaves silverbeet
2 cups vegetable oil
1 leek
sea salt flakes
cracked black pepper

Olive Tapenade
30g black olives, about a good handful, drained of brine
¼ cup extra virgin olive oil

Anchovy Mayonnaise
150ml grapeseed oil
50ml extra virgin olive oil
30ml verjuice
30ml sherry vinegar
30ml lemon juice
10 anchovy fillets
2 free-range organic eggs
2 tablespoons chives, chopped
1 bulb garlic, roasted
a few sprigs of dill and chervil

method

Anchovy Mayonnaise
Preheat oven to 180°C. Take eggs out of fridge and bring to room temperature. Cut garlic bulb and rub with a little olive oil, then place on tray in oven for 45 minutes or until the bulb has turned dark brown and the garlic has softened. Remove and squeeze garlic from bulb. Reserve. In salted water, boil eggs for 2 minutes, then cool in an ice bath. Blend grapeseed and extra virgin olive oils until mixed, then pour into jug and reserve.

Crack and scrape out eggs into food processor or bowl. Add roasted garlic, anchovies, verjuice, sherry vinegar, lemon juice and blend until paste is smooth. Slowly drizzle oils into paste until a thick mayonnaise emulsifies. If you're using a food processor, keep the speed on slow; if you're mixing by hand, make sure you stir constantly - a good trick is to keep your mixing bowl on a wet tea-towel for grip. Add salt and pepper to taste, and a little more lemon juice if necessary. If you accidentally curdle the mayo and it starts to separate, don't worry! You can always save it by using an additional egg yolk and 2 tablespoons of hot water. Top anchovy mayonnaise with a little olive oil to prevent skin forming in an airtight container in fridge for up to 2 days.

Olive Tapenade
Pit black olives by placing stem side down on chopping board, then removing flesh. Blend until smooth with olive oil.

Crispy Silverbeet and Leeks
Wash silverbeet and de-vein by placing leaves face down on a chopping board and removing the white stems with a sharp knife. Cut de-veined silverbeet into 10cm lengths and about 5mm wide. Wash and trim leeks by removing green part and end bulb. Cut leeks into 6cm lengths and remove core. Cut leek into 10cm lengths and about 5mm wide. Heat oil in deep fryer or deep frypan until oil is hot, about 180°C. Deep-fry silverbeet ribbons until crispy - they should start to darken in colour and take on a shiny sheen. Be careful! If you undercook them, they'll be soggy and oily; if you overcook them, they'll be too bitter. Drain silverbeet ribbons on kitchen paper and season with salt while still hot.

Deep-fry leek until crispy, then drain on kitchen paper as for silverbeet ribbons but season with salt and pepper.

Heat fry pan on high heat until screaming hot. Season kingfish fillets with cracked black pepper and salt. Add one tablespoon of oil to hot pan and fry kingfish on all sides for 20 seconds. Remove from pan and rest for 1 minute - this'll make it much easier to slice! Slice each kingfish fillet into 5 equal slices.

To Serve, place 1 tablespoon of anchovy mayonnaise in centre of plate. Place 1 tablespoon of olive tapenade around mayonnaise border. Place silverbeet ribbons on mayo in equal quantities, about 3 tablespoons each. Place kingfish on top of silverbeet and mayo. Place 1 teaspoon of leek ribbons on top of kingfish, then garnish with a few sprigs of dill and chervil.

Margan Family Winegrowers
and Restaurant and Tasting Room
1238 Milbrodale Road
Broke, Hunter Valley NSW 2330
Ph: 02 6579 1372
cellardoor@margan.com.au
www.margan.com.au

Racine @ La Colline

Shaun and Willa Arantz

'Living in Sydney, I think I got a little over confident,' says award-winning chef Shaun Arantz of his start in professional cooking. 'Like most Sydneysiders, I thought Sydney was the best place in the world. Then I got to London...'

It was an education, with an 'exciting time' in hell's kitchen itself, Chelsea's The Admiral Codrington, one of Gordon Ramsay's first gastro-pubs, and opening the acclaimed The White Horse for famous French celebrity chef Jean-Christophe Novelli in the picturesque Hertfordshire countryside, developing close relationships with local hunters, growers and producers, as well as a keener understanding and appreciation of fresh local ingredients.

After three years in the Old Dart, Shaun and his wife Willa were visited by an old family friend who came all the way from Orange with an offer. They'd just built a restaurant on their vineyard, and would Shaun and the equally accomplished Willa (whose extensive hospitality and marketing experience helped Sydney's Cargo Bar win the Australian Hotel Association's coveted Best Marketed Hotel in Australia) come and start the restaurant that would become the successful and acclaimed Schoolhouse?

'We felt we'd paid our dues in the United Kingdom,' says Shaun, 'and we wanted to start our own business, so it was a fantastic opportunity. We jumped straight in - we were in Orange a few days later. We'd always wanted to come here because of the wine and the quality of the produce, and because we wanted to be part of a community, especially of growers, producers and restaurateurs, so we could get to know them and their produce intimately. It's the best thing we've ever done - there's such a strong food community and culture here, and all the growers and producers and restaurateurs are all good friends. It's a really exciting time, and a really wonderful place.'

But although The Schoolhouse did so well it earned its first Sydney Morning Herald Good Food Guide Chef's Hat in its first year, its intimate thirty five covers didn't allow for any further expansion and when the opportunity came up for a larger place closer to town, Shaun and Willa decided to move and start from scratch.

That "start from scratch" is now the award-winning Racine @ La Colline Restaurant, focussing on the best local produce, a huge selection of local wines, encapsulating in Shaun's exceptional food and Willa's wonderful service, the best of Orange.

Racine - that's an interesting name. How did you come up with it?
Well, it's a combination of three things: firstly, it was the name of our favourite little local restaurant in London; it fits its setting, the wonderful La Colline Vineyard, owned by a lovely French couple, Aline and Philippe Prudhomme; and "racine" means "origins" or "roots," which, reflects my passion for fresh, seasonal, local produce and ingredients and our return to the same close kind of rural community in which we were both brought up.

Tell us about The Hundred Mile Diet.
Despite preconceptions of British cuisine, the food culture in the United Kingdom was really exciting, far surpassing Australia's, with people having a much better idea of using local produce and ingredients. Even at The Admiral Codrington in the middle of London, a game farmer would turn up in the morning in his shooting gear - typical tweed suit and wellies, that sort of thing - and take me over to

a Range Rover full of pigeons he'd shot that morning. Experiencing those things in London was quite strange, but then in Hertfordshire we had farmers coming in with deer they'd shot just minutes ago. We don't exactly do that here, but we can have a similar relationship with our local growers and suppliers. And the Hundred Mile Diet (based on the 2007 Canadian book The Hundred Mile Diet: A Year of Eating Locally by Alisa Smith and J.B. MacKinnon) encourages that close relationship by ensuring that everything's sourced from within, well, a hundred miles, so you're always buying locally and seasonally.

And now every restaurant in Orange seems to be following that same sustainable, local Hundred Mile Diet! Did you have to convince them, or did they come quietly?
[laughs] Well, those that weren't basically just followed suit. But the Hundred Mile Diet's only a recent phenomenon, and actually sourcing and eating locally or growing self-sustainably was something that was already happening here. But now the term's become so popular, people are always asking where the produce is from, who produced it, whether it's local. We started a sticker system where we'd put a little apple next to those dishes that used more than 75% local ingredients, for our customers' information. Anyway, there was a time when all the non-stickered items weren't selling as well, and when I quizzed my staff about what was going on, they told me that the customers only wanted local ingredients - which was just fantastic, and made me even more convinced to make the menu completely local.

Aside from the energy and carbon savings through limiting food miles, have you implemented any other green food ideas at Racine @ La Colline?
We're always trying to get it better and looking at ways to reduce our impact on the environment! We're in the process of reducing our water consumption, with rainwater tanks and grey water systems for our kitchen garden, from which we source a lot of our herbs and veggies. And, given the size of the last bill, we're definitely looking into solar power...

How does seasonality affect your menu?
We've got a basic menu which we work around, but it really does depend on what food's available at any time, so sometimes the menu will stay the same for a few months, and sometimes it'll change several times in a week. It keeps things interesting!

Do you think food quality's become better or worse in the past twenty years?
I'd say it used to be a lot worse: it was very basic and there wasn't much variety. It's a lot lot better now. Even though people may think it's hard to cook fresh from scratch, I'd say it's actually a lot easier today to buy something fresh and make something simple, easy and delicious - in fact, as easy if not easier than to reheat some of the awful ready meals.

There's heaps more choice and much more variety - and no excuse not to eat well!

Now, what would you say to anyone inspired by the example of celebrity chefs such as yourself, who wants to take up the pans?
It's like anything - the rich and famous are few and far between (and I wouldn't consider myself one of them!). If you don't have 110 percent interest and passion, then don't bother, because with the exhausting work, sometimes intense pressure and long hours, if you can't put your heart and soul into it, you'll hate it. Whatever impressions of the industry you might get from the telly aren't really accurate about what it's really like. Honestly? It's hard and it's hot, but you get to cook beautiful food that makes people happy, and if everything gels, it's a wonderful feeling - and the reason I do it!

Venue

In its bucolic home in the picturesque Orange vineyard of La Colline, less than a ten minute drive from town, Racine @ La Colline, with the talented Willa's warm enthusiasm filling the elegant dining room, and her beautiful paintings hanging on the mint-green walls side by side with the work of her best and oldest friend Doll's dad, acclaimed artist Pete Wright; with arcadian rural views from the expansive windows and Shaun's exciting French and Modern Australian cuisine on the plate, deserves Restaurant and Catering NSW's prestigious 2010 Best Restaurant in a Winery Award.

Central Western NSW's bread and fruit basket and a leisurely, picturesque three hour drive through some of the country's most spectacular scenery, Orange has always enjoyed its food, from apples, pears, peaches, plums, honey, hazelnuts and mushrooms to more exotic European delicacies like venison and petit-gris snails. And, along with a burgeoning viniculture, a rich food culture, with the green food philosophies of fresh, local, sustainable, simple and slow-cooked green food creating a close community of growers, producers, restaurateurs - and diners.

Since its establishment in 2009 Racine @ La Colline's enjoyed rave reviews from critics and patrons alike, all of them equally enjoying Shaun and Willa's sophisticated approach to food and wine: from The Weekend Australian's Global Gourmet, Australian Gourmet Traveller (which named Racine @ La Colline one of Australia's Top Ten Rural Restaurants) and Vogue Australia (which called dining there one of its Top Fifty Fashionable Experiences) to ecstatic diners who regularly email gushing thanks like this: "The food was amazing, quite simply the best duck I have ever eaten, and combined with your floor staff on the night, made the evening one of best dining experiences we can remember for a long time!"

In addition to their many accomplishments on canvas and in the kitchen, and their passionate championing of Orange produce and producers, Shaun and Willa are passionate about "supporting local" in every aspect of their community. Willa's donated her ample artistic talents to helping the area's small local schools, helping kids focus on and express their pride in their local area. Shaun's got plans for little cooking classes, especially on getting kids into the kitchen early and getting them excited about cooking for themselves. And somehow, in the midst of all this, they've also found the time to make their own line of Racine Kitchen patisserie products, made from local ingredients and sold in local shops, keep a fascinating blog - and bring their first child, Edward, into the world.

Food and Ingredients
Reflecting his Hundred Mile Diet ethos,

nearly every dish on Racine @ La Colline's exciting and intriguing French and Modern Australian menu gets the little apple sticker indicating that at least 75% of its ingredients are locally sourced

- something the menu celebrates by mentioning some of its dedicated local growers and producers, such as Mandagery Creek Venison, Mayfield Beef, Farm Gate Apples, Four Jay Hazelnuts, Huntley Berry Farm and herbs and vegetables from La Colline itself. Much of the fruit and veg is so fresh, it comes off the back of a farmer's truck with the earth still on it!

Seasonally inspired and ever changing, you'll enjoy tempting treats like Venison Tartare with Mushroom Miso Jelly, Bean Sprouts and Pea Shoots; or Celeriac and Mushroom Lasagna with Buckwheat and Spelt Muesli. Enticing mains could include rich and warming Sous Vide Beef Rump with Bone Marrow Purée, Onion Caramel and Glazed Baby Carrots; or simply and beautifully Pan-Roasted Jew Fish with Cauliflower Purée, Blackened Shallot with Cherry Vinegar and Truffle Jus.

'I'd love everything to be local,' laughs Shaun, 'but while landlocked Orange (over 250 kilometres from Shaun's Sydney-based fishmonger) might be famous for a lot of great produce, it isn't famous for seafood.' Along with a small selection of cheeses and chocolate, it's basically the only ingredient that isn't local, although Shaun's at pains to ensure he's in almost daily contact with Frank at De Costi Seafoods and that any fish used is plentiful.

It's not only this close relationship with the land, its produce and its producers that makes Shaun's cooking so exceptional; it's the sensitive and accomplished way he allows these fresh, beautiful ingredients to sing for themselves in classic French and Modern Australian dishes which tip a hat to tradition as they dance in exhilarating new directions. Like Racine @ La Colline's delectable desserts, including Steamed Carrot Pudding with Ginger Jubes and Cream Cheese Sorbet, the tantalising bite of the ginger perfectly complementing the sweet and creamy textures of the pudding and sorbet; or the perfectly Poached Quince with English Breakfast Tapioca, Olive Oil Biscuit and Taleggio Icecream, a gastronomic symphony of textural and taste contrasts and ironies.

'Just because the setting's rural doesn't mean the food has to be rustic,' says Shaun of his deft balance between letting the ingredients shine with as little interference as possible and offering innovative and daring techniques like sous vide cooking or witty takes on the classics, like his Perigord Ham and Pea Consommé, an intriguing twist on pea and ham soup. 'The trick,' he says, 'is to only use those exciting methods, as pioneered by the likes of El Bulli's Ferran Adria or Fat Duck's Heston Blumenthal, when they best serve the dish, and don't threaten the ingredients' integrity.'

Venison with Spring Pea Purée and Soft Boiled Quail's Egg

serves four as a main

ingredients

Spring Pea Purée
1 cup shelled peas or ½ cup frozen peas
4 shallots, finely chopped
3 stems lemon thyme
2 garlic cloves, chopped
100ml veal stock
200ml milk, enough to cover peas in pot
1 tablespoon olive oil
1 tablespoon butter

Venison
1kg venison leg steak
1 tablespoon butter
1 tablespoon olive oil
salt
pepper

Soft Boiled Quail's Egg
4 quail's eggs
1L salted water

method

Spring Pea Purée
Shell peas and reserve some raw peas (about 2 tablespoons) for garnish. Reserve pods for Spring Pea Purée - if you're using frozen peas, you can cook them directly, but keep 2 tablespoons for garnish by defrosting them in the fridge until they're needed - don't cook them! Defrosting in the fridge is good for the fridge, helping to cool it down and keep it running efficiently. Take garnish from fridge about 20 minutes before you plate up.

Finely chop shallots and garlic. Heat olive oil or butter in frypan and gently sweat shallots and garlic for 2 minutes or until soft. Add peas and thyme, then enough milk and stock to cover peas. Gently bring to simmer but not boiling for 30 seconds.

Check peas are done, then remove pan from heat. Leave for 10 minutes to let flavours infuse. Strain off liquid and reserve. In a blender, purée peas and pea pods, slowly adding reserved liquid until it makes a smooth paste.

Venison
Slice venison with the grain lengthways into 4 equal pieces. Lightly season venison with salt, pepper and olive oil, then sear venison in frypan for 30 seconds on each side.

To cook venison medium rare, place all pieces on a baking tray in a hot oven at 250°C for 6 to 8 minutes.

Check venison at 6 minutes to see if it's cooked. An easy way to check is to place a sheet of baking paper over venison to avoid burning yourself, and by pressing venison in the middle with your finger. If it has a slight firmness to touch, remove from oven and rest for 4 minutes, or half the cooking time. If it still needs a bit more, return to oven for 1 or 2 minutes more then remove and rest.

Soft Boiled Quail's Egg
Remove quail's eggs from refrigerator to raise to room temperature, about 30 minutes before use.

While venison is resting, bring salted water quickly to boil and gently lower quail's into water and boil gently for 2 minutes - you might like to use a teaspoon to do this to avoid the shells cracking. Keep an eye on the time as 2 minutes will fly by like a hungry quail! Once 2 minutes are up, remove eggs and place in cold water for 10 minutes to stop cooking. Once cooled, gently remove the shell and set aside for plating.

To serve, reheat Spring Pea Purée and smear an equal amount on each plate, using the back of a tablespoon by moving dollop from one side of plate to the other. Cut each piece of venison in half across the grain and place on top of spring pea purée. Cut quail's eggs in half lengthways by holding egg gently between index finger and thumb on chopping board. Slice downwards from top of egg slowly and carefully, then gently separate two halves. The yolk should be light yellow and runny. Place halves on plate.

Garnish with fresh raw shelled peas or defrosted frozen peas.

Racine @ La Colline
42 Lake Canobolas Road
Orange NSW 2800
Ph: 02 6365 3275
info@racinerestaurant.com.au
www.racinerestaurant.com.au

La Table Café and Restaurant

Bruno and Louise Pouget

A skilled and talented French chef with an ebullient Aussie personality, Bruno Pouget has as many surprises and contrasts as his exceptional, fresh, light French and Mediterranean-inspired food. A member of Greenpeace, Slow Food and the Australian Maritime Conservation Society, he guiltily admits his last meal would have to be pan-fried goose liver on rye toast with a good ten year old vintage of Château d'Yquiem. 'It would be my last meal, after all,' he laughs. But such a simple and sophisticated meal perfectly reflects the unalloyed and beautifully done dishes at his and his equally talented wife Louise's popular restaurant La Table, on NSW's beautiful Far North Coast, which combines French tradition and modern Mediterranean flavours for a uniquely Australian context, culture and climate.

You could say the same of Louise, a Sydney girl with French ancestry, whose résumé reveals a career as interesting and eclectic as the menu. A trained yoga instructor, chef, pasta company manager's personal assistant and with a long history of hospitality here and abroad, her vast experience and skill have proven as invaluable to La Table as it was when she quit her job to follow her heart and join Bruno at his restaurant in Provence, La Table des Vergiers, and later, in the same village, their guesthouse Les Hauts de Veroncle.

Returning to Australia four years ago with their two little girls Lily and Manon, they've found their own little patch of paradise in Mullum (as it's affectionately known by townsfolk) offering locals and visitors alike an evocative and authentic taste of Provence, or as the local newspaper rapturously put it, "Mullumbimby magic with a French accent," drawing on Bruno and Louise's deep convictions about sustainability, slow-food, local and ethical produce - and French flair - to make La Table not only one of the country's most exciting eateries, but its greenest.

How did you two meet?

Louise: How we met? The famous question! [laughs] We met in Greytown, near Wellington on New Zealand's North Island. We had some mutual friends, Moise, a French pâtissier married to a Kiwi girl, Andrea. Both Bruno and I happened to be there when Moise and Andrea were opening their pâtisserie, and we had a holiday romance. Then a long distance relationship for a while, me working in Sydney and Bruno only in the second year of running La Table des Vergiers in Provence. But in the end, I followed my heart and quit my job and went over to join him. We haven't been apart since!

As married chefs running a restaurant together, how do you decide what'll be on the menu?

Louise: Well, we've definitely got different cooking backgrounds. Bruno had very traditional French training whereas my background's more Italian, because it's the style of food I like to cook. My food's more rustic, his style's more refined. So it's interesting, we find a balance between the two - without too many arguments about it! [laughs]

How did your Provençal experience translate to Mullum?

Louise: We brought a lot of things, like the idea of the long communal table. But the most important thing was the slow-food, locally-sourced ethos that's so ingrained in French cooking and the French way of life. Provence is blessed with lots of amazing produce, like wild boar, lentils, grains, olives, goat's cheese, honey and the best fruit and vegetables. And we're really lucky to have found a region with amazing produce and the same kind of green food culture here.

Is there a strong green food culture in Mullumbimby?
Bruno: Yes! We don't have any fast food joints here, and we've got growers' markets four times a week in the district, with a new market in Mullumbimby once a week, which has enjoyed a great deal of community support. We've done cooking demonstrations at one of the farmers' markets to showcase local ingredients and to give shoppers some exciting new ideas for cooking simply at home - it was really popular. And even better, a lot of our growers and suppliers offer to drop produce off to us because they're on their way to market!

What's your relationship with local growers and suppliers?
Louise: Our reputation for appreciating the freshest and best locally-sourced ingredients has grown in the two years since we opened La Table's doors, and we've got lots of local farmers approaching us directly, asking us if we'd like to buy their produce, which we do, if it meets our standards. And we love the close relationships we've developed with a number of them - they are, after all, our neighbours, our community.

How does seasonality and locality affect your menu?
Louise: Well, there are few things we can't get, either because of availability or price. For example, if we wanted a specific cut of pork, like the cheeks, it'd be hard to find locally; and often, because of transport and other costs, a lot of ingredients can be more expensive here than in the city. But along with the little challenges come the much greater pleasures of being in such a fantastically fertile place, the volcanic soil and sub-tropical climate producing some amazing ingredients!

What do you think about organic food?
Bruno: [laughs]

Organic food's normal! For thousands of years, it was the only way to grow food and make wine. It's a weird irony that non-organic food's called "conventional" - it's a total nonsense!

There's more and more evidence that unsustainable non-organic agriculture isn't acceptable anymore - the environmental and health impacts can be disastrous. Organic food isn't just better for you, it tastes better too. Our local wine supplier, The Organic Wine Merchants, offers a diverse range of Australian and Kiwi organic and bio-dynamic wines, and though of course we want to showcase wines that are made from sustainable practices, they're absolutely gorgeous to drink.

Louise: We do try to be an ethical business, living to the philosophies we hold dear, but it's also a matter of what's viable. When we started La Table, we were mostly organic and our food costs went through the roof. So we're always trying to find a balance between what good organic food costs, and what people want to pay. We can't pass all those food costs onto our customers. But we'd love to use more organic food as prices come down.

What factors do you think will help make organic green food more affordable and widespread?

Louise: In a word? Demand. Demand's the only thing that'll lower green food prices.
Bruno: Population's the key to improving food quality and choices. In our highly capitalised society, we're probably more consumers than citizens: after all, isn't the customer supposed to be king? So we should be aware of our power as consumers, because industry only offers what consumers demand and buy.

The more people ask for and expect organic food, the more agribusiness will have to comply

- we can see lots of examples where the law hasn't proven as powerful a motivation.

Having said that, one of our favourite local suppliers, Santos, is active in promoting a large selection of fresh produce and health products that are Certified Organic, genetically modified-free and have a low-carbon footprint. And conscientious businesses like that will always have our community's support.

What green food initiatives have you implemented at La Table?

Louise: We've got a range of measures, including energy-saving light bulbs, eco cleaning products, solar hot water and we send all our kitchen waste to the Mullumbimby Community Garden for composting.
Bruno: And we've been members of Greenpeace, Slow Food, the World Wildlife Fund and currently support the Australian Marine Conservation Society. We could always do more, but we do as much as we can - it's by doing as much as you can that you can make a difference!

Venue

Sitting at the busy communal table, sharing Bruno and Louise's fresh, light, sustainable and ethical modern Mediterranean cuisine, surrounded by the tinkling patter of French and Aussie laughter, you could be forgiven for imagining you were in a slow food paradise. With its temperate sub-tropical weather and easy-going lifestyle, Mullumbimby's as close a slice of Provence as you could find Down Under - especially after one mouthful of Bruno's Omelette Provençal with Ratatouille and Goat's Cheese, that is!

Nestled in the rich volcanic soil of the Brunswick Valley at the foot of the spectacular Mount Chincogan, it's a close and broad-minded community, offering a gentler-paced alternative lifestyle for locals, tree changers and tourists alike. Close to the breathtaking beauty of Cape Byron's world-famous beaches, it's a wonderful home for Bruno, Louise, their young family and their popular, award-winning restaurant, named one of the Top Ten Sustainable Restaurants in NSW by the prestigious 2010 Sydney Morning Herald Good Food Guide.

Whether a lazy breakfast in the bright and buzzy café, or family lunch at the long table in the tropical courtyard, an intimate dinner in the restaurant or a wedding, party or other special function in the café, restaurant or lush gardens, La Table offers something for everyone - sustainably, ethically, locally. 'It's seriously good food,' laughs Bruno. 'But it's also seriously good fun!'

You can even take a little of your La Table experience home with you, with fabulous house-baked cakes and pastries and dairy-free and gluten-free options available.

Food and Ingredients

'Food's about sharing,' says Bruno, and in the café's tropical gardens, you can appreciate and enjoy that simple pleasure, from traditional Australian breakfast favourites like Eggs Benedict with Sautéed Spinach, Smoked Salmon or Ham; French classics like Ham and Cheese Croissants or Bruno's famous Omelette Provençal; or more exotic offerings like Vanilla Bean Pancakes with Raspberries, Cream and Maple Syrup or rich and fragrant Black Sticky Rice with Coconut Cream, Grilled Banana and Passionfruit. For lunch, why not try sunny delights like Zucchini and Haloumi Fritters with Roast Pumpkin, Caramelised Onion, Rocket and Olive Salad; the filling Slow Cooked Bangalow Pork Belly, Warm Chat Potato, Beetroot, Rocket and Caper Salad with Balsamic Reduction; the popular Blue Eye Cod Laksa with Rice Noodles, Coriander Sprouts and Fried Shallots; or La Table's famous Organic Beef Burger on Turkish Bread with Aïoli, Salad, Cheddar Cheese, Beetroot Relish and Caramelised Onions. Sure beats a Big Mac on flavour, freshness, nutrition - and love!

Savour the flavours of this wonderful place at dinner in the adjoining restaurant, with the elegant décor for an intimate dining experience, a perfect match for Bruno's sophisticated fare. If you thought French cuisine was heavy, think again. Reflecting his and Louise's close relationship with the local area and its ingredients, La Table's menu isn't just seasonal, but, using so many regional ingredients, is local as well, with a lightness of touch and delicacy of taste that suits this place and climate so well.

Enjoy a lavish sharing plate in the afternoon over which to linger with a bottle or two of The Organic Wine Merchants' wonderful wines, featuring anything from Escargots Sautéed with Leek, Bacon & Shiraz Butter in Puff Pastry; a Slice of French Cheese with Croutons; or Freshly Shucked Oysters with Golden Shallot & Sherry Vinegar, depending on the season and what's available. Or indulge yourself at dinner with eclectic and enticing entrées like Grilled Spicy Prawns with Avocado Salsa and Paprika Aïoli; or Goat's Cheese Gnocchi with Braised Fennel, Tomato and Golden Pine Nuts; or, for dinner, sweet local Jewfish with Saffron Rice Pilaf, Zucchini and Riesling Beurre Blanc; tender Roast Lamb Rump with Ratatouille, Herb Polenta and Bush Pepper Jus; or Bruno's signature dish, Duck Confit with Carrot and Orange Tartlet, Green Beans and Star Anise Sauce, which will have you swooning with happiness, according to the chef. See if you can stop yourself from sampling both Pougets' pastry expertise, from the intriguing Crème Brulée "au Pastis" to the "Airy Meringue Island" with Mandarin Crème Anglaise.

Whatever you enjoy at La Table, you can do so knowing Bruno and Louise's passion and commitment have ensured that it is as local or organic as possible - or preferably both! Their love and support of their local community is reflected in the extensive use of local ingredients and products, from locally roasted Espresso Botero organic coffee served with Barambah Organics Milk, as well as AJ's Ducks, Bangalow Sweet Pork, Plateau Prestige Certified Free Range Eggs, Jordan's Breads, Summerland Olives and more.

Duck Confit with Five Spice and Shiraz Sauce

serves eight as a main

'This recipe may seem pretty challenging,' says Bruno. 'Many people are daunted by cooking duck, let alone for so long, and it's often something they only order in a restaurant. But people have been cooking confit duck at home in France forever, so it's not that hard! Try this, get to know the subtle flavours and the pure joy of slow-cooking something for half a day - once you've put everything in the oven, just sit back, relax and let the mouth-watering scent of roasting duck fill your home while you get ready for dinner. And watch your friends drool and sigh with joy when you bring it to the table!'

ingredients

Duck
4 whole ducks, weighing about 2kg each
2kg duck fat, from your butcher or provedore
420g salt
65g sugar

Duck Sauce
4 remaining duck frames
500ml shiraz
50ml cognac
3L water, enough to cover all ingredients
4 carrots, unpeeled
3 onions
1 large celery stick
1 small leek
½ cup runny honey
¼ whole black peppercorns
20g coriander seeds
8 cloves
8 star anises
6 juniper berries
5 tomatoes
2 bay leaves
2 cinnamon sticks
1 thyme sprig
1 rosemary sprig
1 garlic bulb

method

Duck Meat
Using a sharp knife, remove legs and breasts from duck, or get your butcher to do this for you if you're not sure. Freeze breasts for future use. Mix salt and sugar and spread enough over duck legs to evenly coat. Refrigerate duck legs for at least 2 hours.

Remove duck legs from fridge and put in a baking tray. Cover with duck fat and cover tray with lid or foil. Cook in oven for 12 hours at 85°C.

Duck Sauce
Preheat oven to 220°C. While duck legs are marinating, remove as much meat as you can from duck frames and reserve.

Put duck frames in oven tray and roast for 40 minutes until bones are golden. Roughly chop carrots, onions, celery, leek and tomatoes and cut garlic bulb in half, leaving skin on. Add all sauce ingredients except wine and cognac and keep roasting for 10 minutes until everything's dark and caramelised.

Remove from oven and put everything in a deep pot or stockpot. You may prefer to use a crockpot or slow cooker instead to avoid leaving open flames or elements unattended.

Deglaze baking tray with shiraz and ½ cup of water on high heat on stove, then add scrapings and sauce to pot. Fill pot with cold water to cover bones. Cook on stove top at extremely low temperature for 5 hours (or in crockpot or slow cooker for 12 hours). Strain and reduce on high heat until rich and glazed.

Add cognac to taste - if the sauce is too rich, add a dash of balsamic vinegar.

Serve with your favourite stewed vegetables baked in a short pastry tart and a good bottle of pinot noir, like The Thistle Hill Mudgee Pinot Noir 2006, an organic wine on La Table's list Bruno thinks is the perfect match - and enjoy with friends and family!

La Table Café and Restaurant
72 Burringbar Street
Mullumbimby NSW 2482
Café: 02 6684 2220
Restaurant: 02 6684 2227
contact@latable.com.au
www.latable.com.au

South Bank Surf Club

Ben "Bender" O'Donoghue

You'd recognise Ben O'Donoghue - "Bender" to his mates - from his many acclaimed television series, including BBC2's The Best, the Food Network's Planet Food, or closer to home, Surfing the Menu with his mates Curtis Stone and Mark Gardner. He's had a career as wide as his travels, and a long way from his start after school as a part-time kitchen hand on the holiday resort of Rottnest Island, off the beautiful West Australian coast, intending to chase his three biggest passions at the time: 'Surfing, women and, uh, surfing,' he laughs.

But it was working at Jo Jo's on the Jetty in Perth's Nedlands that he discovered his passion for cooking, and took up an apprenticeship before moving onto Sydney's two-hatted Goodfellas Restaurant and heading to London, where he worked with some of the world's greatest chefs, like Ruth Rogers and the late Rose Gray at the famed River Café; and working in some of the capital's best restaurants, including opening the acclaimed Monte's at Knightsbridge with fellow River Café alumnus Jamie Oliver. Reflecting his endless curiosity and energy, he ended up being head-hunted by London's famous Atlantic Bar and Grill, before embarking on his wildly successful television career.

But after thirteen years overseas and on the road, authoring numerous books and cooking for countless celebrities, Bender took a breather, returning to his homeland and establishing the first restaurant he'd call his own: the relaxed and welcoming South Bank Surf Club, reflecting his laidback charm and passion for sustainable, local, green food and seafood.

From Knightsbridge to South Brisvegas is a bit of a leap! Why did you start your restaurant here?

Look around you! The first moment I saw the view of the city over the river and this beautiful man-made beach, I just knew I'd found the ideal place. Having done the fine-dining thing for other chefs and celebrities, I wanted to start my own place, but I wanted something fun and relaxed, like the surf clubs I missed when I was back in Blighty. We've tried to give it that classic surf club feel, including taking that traditional surf club menu and giving it a funky twist - like "surfing up" your char-grilled, grass-fed Barcoo Darling Downs Angus X Ribeye with a juicy Garlic Cajun Bug. Mmmm…

Updating the classics aside, how have you implemented your own green food goals at the Southbank Surf Club?

Running my own place, I really wanted to take a lead in implementing structures that would limit our environmental impact. We only source sustainably produced seafood and local ingredients where we can, and limit the amount of packaging that comes through the kitchen. One thing that does discourage a lot of people from making that effort, especially when establishing their business, is that because the technology is new and not widespread yet, it can be a bit prohibitive. So we've started a pilot program with Brisbane City Council to get all the restaurants and food businesses on the South Bank involved in the recycling of their green, organic and kitchen waste. We've also got a kitchen garden that'll use a lot of this compost waste to hopefully grow interesting things to supplement the menu.

Is the kitchen garden on-site?

Yeah! We've got about six or seven large planters that form the building's super-structure, and during construction we filled them with soil and some compost. I'm looking forward to growing some interesting, hard-to-get things in there - like, say, heritage tomatoes and herbs - so we can supplement the menu and offer some unique specials.

Why would you take a green food approach to business, given the additional costs?
Having been involved in the industry since 1987 - has it really been that long? - you do become adept at managing waste and processes. It might be a bit more expensive during initial start up but the marketing point of difference is terrific. For some time now, people have been moving towards more environmentally-aware dining. It started with organic food, but it's developing into a broader sort of concern with how food is produced and the amount that's wasted - apparently, nearly forty percent of food's wasted in Australia, just chucked into landfill.

Confucius said that "the journey of a thousand miles begins with one step." And that journey's preserving the environment for our children and our children's children.

If we could either stop wasting food, or else harness that waste in a circular system, so that we can recycle that waste into compost, we can take that important first step, and we'd be a good way down that path.

Do you have any pet peeves about the food industry?
Packaging! Everything nowadays seems to be cling wrapped three or four times, in needless extra bags, on polyurethane trays… the energy that must go into making all that extra plastic, let alone wrapping it, let alone disposing of it! Whatever happened to brown paper bags, biodegradable and easy?

A lot of people say the biggest challenge to making green food more popular in Australia is the size of the market. Would a bigger population help that?
Probably not - I mean, look at America or China! It's been said that you'd save more emissions by eating red meat once a week instead of every night, than limiting yourself to local produce. We do need to really have a close look at how and what we consume - perhaps making red meat an occasion, like it was in the past, for the Sunday roast. We'd be more likely to celebrate and respect it, demanding the best, rather than blindly consuming substandard meat or derivative products.

We should definitely be eating more veggies than red meat - not just from a health perspective but from an environmental one: vegetables return far more to the soil and require far less energy and water than red meat production does, although obviously, when it's done ethically, and not dependant on exorbitant amounts of pesticides and fertilisers.

What do you think about organic food, then?

In theory, I reckon organic food's fantastic, especially environmentally. Unfortunately, in reality, I'm not sure, given how stringent certification is, that a lot of people are growing in a certified way, so I think a lot of it's just a marketing ploy. And unfortunately, although it'd be nice to use organic food all the time, it's just a bit too expensive from a business perspective, so it's really a matter of finding that balance between quality, price and demand.

Do you factor in food miles when sourcing produce?

To a degree, but it's all about balances and compromises. Australia's a big country with big distances and I don't think you can restrict yourself to an arbitrary 150 kilometre limit - it's a bit naïve to think you can have a diverse, creative or appealing menu with a very limited number of ingredients. For example, yes, I can get Queensland strawberries, but so can Melbourne chefs; but I'd always buy Aussie over an imported equivalent. For example,

I'd never consider using Italian buffalo mozzarella when the Australian product is so good!

So what green food generational things are you most proud of at South Bank Surf Club?

It'd have to be this exciting new group system we're starting up to recycle our green waste. We'll be collecting every scrap of organic waste and sending it off to get composted. Eventually, we'd like to get all of Brisbane's CBD involved, sending in its organic waste to be composted so that the whole city can use this wonderful, recycled compost and cut down on landfill. And, closer to home, I'd love to establish a totally green South Bank community spice garden, where kids could come down and learn all about galangal, kaffir lime trees and other exotic and exciting spices. It'd be fantastic!

Venue

Like this confident city itself, the Brisbane restaurant scene is booming, and nowhere's busier or buzzier than the South Bank Surf Club. Set on the sands of Brisbane's hip South Bank cultural precinct, its sunny setting reflects its relaxed Aussie attitude to life, with a fun and informal al fresco dining area looking out over Streets Beach and its man-made beach pool, Brisbane River and the rapidly growing city skyline. 'But just because we're relaxed,' says Ben, 'doesn't mean we cut corners - the setting may be casual, the vibe laidback, but the food and service are the very best!'

In addition to the main restaurant, there's a funky bar, serving a wide range of wine, cocktails and that great Aussie staple, ice cold beer - over sixteen different to choose from, and ideal for a session as you watch the world go by - accompanied by some of Ben's famous Wasabi Prawns or more-ish Salt and Pepper Calamari with Lime Mayo.

Welcoming everyone from families and couples to corporates and the kids, Ben and his collaborator, well-known Brisbane hospitality identity Bevan Bickle, want to encourage that surf club vibe by creating a community of locals. Occasionally, Ben encourages locals to be his guinea pigs as he cooks up some exciting nibbles on the house at always-popular "Come Down and Meet Ben O'Donoghue" events.

Join up to the South Bank Surf Club's Socials pages and you'll be part of the club, enjoying the latest news, special offers, exclusive events and birthday freebies in their exclusive newsletter, The Surf Report. Sign up at www.southbanksurfclub.com.au/social.htm.

Food and Ingredients

It's like surf club cordon bleu! Drawing on the surf club classics he loved growing up and the gourmet delights he served to some of the world's best-known celebrities in some of London's best and best-known restaurants, Bender gives Aussie favourites a modern . 'It's like Brisbane - tradition with a twist!' he says. Given its tropical setting and surf club theme, seafood is a major part of the South Bank Surf Club menu. Ben's passion for sustainable and ethical green food means he'll only use Queensland produce where possible and sustainably fished varieties with fast growth cycles, like the bream in his Daily Surf Report specials such as Whole Thai-Grilled Fish with Green Papaya Salad and Sticky Rice; or the mullet roe he uses in his home-made Taramasalata.

Of course, you can always enjoy the Chicken Snizzer, Bender's own chicken schnitzel sandwich with juicy cornflake-crumbed juicy chicken breast served smothered with Salsa Rossa Picante, Sage, Rosemary and Anchovy Burnt Butter; or the Surf Club Open Steak Sandwich, a generous slab of steak served on sourdough with Onion Confit and Bender's Béarnaise. If you can get past Daily Surf Report specials, like Wednesday Stir Fried Chilli Blue Swimmer Crab with House made XO sauce and Chilli Vermicelli egg noodles; or Thursday's Jambayala, a Cajun-style Paella with chorizo, prawns, crabs, mussels and oysters; or Daily Surf Report: Saturday - Whole Grilled Thai Style Reef Fish served with green papaya salad and sticky rice.

The Surf Club isn't an exclusive club, and much of its menu is made for sharing, including the lavish Long Board for Two, featuring the Surf Club's famous Anti Pasti, including crudité and roasted local in-season vegetables, Chicken Liver Parfait, a creamy and extra-specially smooth pâté, Vanella buffalo mozzarella and baked ricotta. Or the Boogey Board for Two, featuring Bender's selection of sourdough bruschetta, grilled marinated pepper, Vannella buffalo mozzarella, salumi and basil. And in the Crustacean Bar, indulge in The Duke, a lavish sharing spread of the best hot and cold seafood, including beautiful tiger prawns, sweet Moreton Bay bugs, deep-fried whiting and calamari, oysters natural and Kilpatrick and Pineapple Spadino, a summery skewer of bug, pancetta and pineapple.

Not just a great place to meet someone special for dinner, the Surf Club offers Brisvegas's best weekend brekkie, including Surf Club Crumble Pots, stewed seasonal fruits with Vannella buffalo yoghurt and granola crumble; Eggs Bender, featuring Snowy Morrison's famous hot smoked salmon, poached free-range eggs, horseradish hollandaise on a potato hotcake; or, for the more adventurous (and possibly hung-over), the Surf Club Classic, a fiery heart starter of grilled Gold Coast tiger prawns, smoked bacon, deep fried egg, oyster sauce and fresh chilli on a corn and coriander hot cake. Got room for pudding? How about the Surf Club Knickerbocker that'll knock your pants off? Or Bender's favourite, the decadent Chocolate Nemesis, a signature dish from his River Café days, a rich flourless chocolate that he says 'is more like the most wicked chocolate mousse you've ever tasted. Ever!'

Wasabi Prawns in Angel Hair with Mango and Watermelon Salad

serves four as an entrée

This fresh, tasty and spicy delight combines good old Aussie prawns with Asian flavours and a fruity salad. The combination of sweet, salty and spicy flavours makes for an interesting and tantalising meal, celebrating the best of Australia's bountiful summer.

Kadayif is a fine, shredded Turkish filo pastry, used for making the delicacy künefe. You can get it from good Middle Eastern or Turkish delis and specialty gourmet provedores, although more and more major supermarkets are stocking it in the frozen aisle, according to Ben. 'I love Japanese mayonnaise, like Kewpie,' says Ben, 'which you can get - along with wasabi - in any Asian grocery or the Asian foods section of your supermarket, but any good, whole-egg mayonnaise is fine.'

ingredients

Wasabi Prawns and Angel Hair
12 "16 and Under" fresh green tiger prawns
12 wooden skewers
500ml peanut oil
4 tablespoons Japanese mayonnaise (like Kewpie)
3 teaspoons wasabi paste
half a packet of kadayif pastry

Mango and Watermelon Salad
2 ripe Bowen or Kingston Pride mangoes, cut into 1 cm cubes - you can use red papaya if mango's unavailable
2 thick wedges watermelon, cut into 1cm cubes
half a bunch of coriander, washed and picked
2 limes
1 long red chilli, julienned

method

Cut mango and watermelon into 1cm cubes. Reserve.

Peel and de-vein prawns, leaving tail on, then thread onto skewers - it's a lot easier to roll the prawns in the kadayif with the skewers on. Combine mayonnaise with half the wasabi, then dress plate with several dollops of wasabi mayonnaise.

Arrange mango and watermelon cubes around plate - in an artistic fashion, of course! Smear each prawn tail with remaining wasabi. Lay out kadayif pastry and roll prawn tails in filo strands.

Fry prawn skewers in hot peanut oil for 2 minutes, or until pastry's a lovely light golden-brown then drain prawn skewers on kitchen paper, season with salt and pepper and serve on top of wasabi mayonnaise dollops.

Garnish with coriander leaves, julienned red chilli and a wedge of lime.

green tips

Watch what you waste
Start a food refuse bin at home and just see how much food you throw away - better yet, start a compost bin or worm farm and put that waste to good use!

Grow a green thumb
Put that compost or those worm casings from above to good use by growing your own fruit and veggies - nothing tastes better than home-grown! If you don't have the space, why not start a little herb garden? You'll always have your favourite fresh herbs on demand!

Do little shops
What's the point of shopping in bulk, if everything just ends up wasted? Shop regularly for fresh fruit, veggies, meat and fish in smaller quantities, so you'll use fresher, seasonal ingredients, get to know your providores - and just see how much more innovative and inventive your meals will become!

Southbank Surf Club
30a Stanley Plaza
Parklands
South Brisbane, QLD 4101
Ph: 07 3844 7301
info@southbanksurfclub.com.au
www.southbanksurfclub.com.au

Red meat production can release as much carbon as a car in a year. And that's not counting the water usage, soil degradation, transport and refrigeration involved! If you just reduce your red meat consumption by one meal a week, you can do more to reduce carbon emissions than reducing food miles. Meat was a treat in the past, and people traditionally ate far more vegetables, grains and legumes, a far healthier and more natural diet. When you do buy meat, make sure it's as green as all your food.

Ochre Restaurant and Catering

Craig Squire

Craig Squire spent the early years of his career travelling around Australia, and his experiences and understanding of the country and its different cuisines are reflected in the exciting and eclectic dishes on offer at his renowned Ochre Restaurant in beautiful sun-kissed Cairns in Tropical North Queensland.

In 1994, after working in some of Australia and the world's best restaurants from London's The Orangery Restaurant at Kensington Place with legendary Albert and Michel Roux of Le Gavroche fame and a stint in the Michelin-starred restaurant of Austria's famous Sporthotel Reisch, Craig's success with the award-winning Red Ochre Restaurant in Adelaide led him to creating the then Red Ochre in Cairns. Specialising in the modern, indigenous Australian cuisine he helped to pioneer, Craig's menu offers diners from around Australia and the world a rare authentic taste of Australia.

In addition to running one of Cairns' best known and best loved restaurants, Craig's also employed his vast knowledge of regional produce and its potential to help establish Australian Tropical Foods, a Government-sponsored industry group dedicated to promoting the regional food industry which, after thirteen years of hard work and commitment, has culminated in the launch of Taste Paradise, Tropical North Queensland's own exciting regional food brand, showcasing the best of the region's abundant bounty, and featuring inspiring recipes from Craig and some of its best chefs. Find out more at http://www.tasteparadise.com.au.

Like macadamias and kangaroo fillet and the best of Aussie bush tucker, Craig himself has become an Australian green food export, called upon to present the best of Australia on a plate, with his innovative approach to Australian ingredients representing regions, States and the nation around the world. Now re-branded as Ochre Restaurant and Catering, his thriving business continues to be a Cairns tourist landmark - and a green food benchmark.

What are your opinions about bush tucker, as opposed to more conventional sustainable green food methods?
When people talk about sustainability in the food industry, they usually mention things like dual flush toilets or slow flow taps. But really, these things only have a minor effect on energy use. My attitude's that by using Australian native foods you're doing a lot more for sustainability, because Australian native foods don't require fertilisers, extra water, pesticides, they're in harmony with the Australian environment.

When we talk about things like kangaroo meat, the benefits aren't just environmental - although it's great that kangaroos require far less grain, grass or water than cattle, and make much less impact on the topsoil, and with their high protein and low fat content, they're ridiculously good for you. And they taste fantastic!

People tend to shy away from kangaroo because they think of Skippy. But perhaps Hindus in India would be shocked at our obsession with beef...

Yeah! Have you ever looked into a cow's big, long-lashed eyes? [laughs]. But their cuteness aside, cows fart an enormous volume of greenhouse gases like methane and carbon dioxide. Queensland's Darling Downs produce more emissions than many Australian cities! So you've got these creatures which require huge amounts of food and water, which itself has generally been transported long distances, and that steak on your plate has cost more in carbon emissions and miles than you could stomach. Kangaroos, on the other hand, are soft-hoofed so they don't impact on the soil, they don't require much water, and they can live easily and naturally off the land.

What about crocodile? Is that a sustainable food?

Sure, for a number of reasons. They don't take up much room. If they're farmed, the bulk of their diet is old, poor quality broiler chook, which would otherwise have been chucked out or processed into fertiliser. And they don't fart like cows, so they don't release a lot of emissions. The water they live in is usually recycled estuary water which is re-filtered and put back into the river system. And because they're locally grown and slaughtered, they don't require much transport.

What indigenous ingredients or bush tucker do you use in your cooking?

We use a whole bunch of bush foods, locally-grown and from around Australia. Locally, we've got lemon aspen, Davidson plums, lemon myrtle, native tamarind, rosella flowers and wild finger limes. Further afield, you've got desert limes, bush tomatoes, quandongs, wattle seed. Obviously, Australia's a big country, so some of these ingredients need a bit of transport, but not as much as if they were imported from overseas.

What can you source locally?

We get a fair bit of local chicken, beef, pork. Of course, being right on the Barrier Reef, the seafood is amazing. We've been getting some awesome leader prawns - fresh, local, organic, wild and enormous! The more sustainable you get, the more local you get, the more you've got to be subject to seasonality, and the more flexibility you've got to have on the menu. Most restaurants in Australia probably use prawns and asparagus throughout the year. And the chefs don't even think about the fact that they're probably imported most of the year. My seafood suppliers tell me that about seventy-five percent of the restaurants they supply are using imported prawns from India or Thailand - mostly grown in sewerage. I've had this restaurant since 1994 and I've never used an imported prawn.

Is there a lot of confusion about the origin of such produce?

Well, a lot of chefs and people just shop by price. I think Australia's still pretty poor when it comes to making purchasing distinctions about the country of origin. I don't think we've got enough balls when it comes to legislation for labelling. It's there, but it's not strong enough.

Could Australia have its own sustainable fishing industry?
In Queensland - if we keep fishing at the current rate - seafood can be self-sustainable. Being mindful to encourage certain fishing practices is important, though. On the whole, if you couldn't import overseas products, I think Australia would develop its aquaculture more. But, more importantly, naturally the price would go up. And that's actually something that would do both the environment and our fishing industry both a lot of good, because trying to compete with these cheap imports forces the Australian industry's prices and profits down anyway.

But in comparison to the other costs involved in running Ochre Restaurant and the Catering business, like other produce, wages or utility bills, it's not a huge premium to pay. Seafood pricing is undervalued - I only pay about $2.50 a kilo more for local prawn cutlets, than imported, and they are much better quality.

What are the benefits of doing what you're doing?
Actually, the number of environmentally-aware restaurant patrons in Cairns is only nominal. Unlike places in Sydney or Melbourne, there's very little marketing advantage in it for me to promote those issues - people come for the food, not the idea (or the sermon!).

By trying to source as much of our produce locally, it benefits and celebrates the community and region. It's a bit more expensive, but worth it.

That's a big contribution you're making to local producers!
Well, it's partly for my own peace of mind, but since we actively started trying to create a local green food movement and establish networking support for restaurateurs and producers with Australian Tropical Foods, it's started to generate its own momentum, letting people know there's a growing market for niche or specialty farming and products, and allowing them to make those connections and get it going.

What do you think are the next big things to happen for the Tropical North Queensland Green Food Generation?
Cacao and chocolate are going to be big. There's also exciting talk about lots of interesting projects, such as establishing an organic zone, where all the produce is certified, and no chemicals are allowed. We've got the biggest food-bowl potential in Australia: we've got constant water, a varied and tropical climate - look around, it's lush!

Venue

For over sixteen years, Ochre Restaurant has offered a fun and intriguing blend of culinary sophistication and natural simplicity. Warm Australian wood and ochre tones offer a welcoming and unpretentious setting for a menu of exceptional quality, imagination and innovation.

Reflecting Craig's passion for indigenous ingredients, Australian cuisine and green food, Ochre Restaurant offers local and tourists a rare taste of Australia - not just in the buzzing dining room, but also via its popular catering business, Ochre Catering, which since 1995 has been catering many of Cairns's most prestigious and popular events - even once serving up in the middle of a cyclone! But their original, healthy and delicious menu can be perfectly tailored to any occasion, from corporate she-bang to intimate dinner.

You can even take a little taste of Ochre Restaurant home, if you purchase any of its

Tropical Spirit handmade in-house bush tucker products, like Pineapple Chilli Jam, a sweet and spicy condiment that's perfect with grilled pork; Native Dukkah, a fragrant blend of local native and imported spices mixed with roasted macadamia and coconut; or delectable Macadamia and Rocket Pesto, which balances the rocket's sharpness with the rich meatiness of locally-grown macadamias. You can also purchase specially prepared native spices, such as ground wattleseed, dried quandongs or fresh lemon-myrtle leaves, either at the restaurant or on-line. And if you're not quite sure how to use them, Craig generously offering some of his most popular recipes on both Ochre Restaurant and Australian Tropical Foods' websites, full of fresh and inspiring ideas.

The proof, as Craig might say, is in the Lemon Myrtle Panna Cotta, winning countless awards, including the Tourism Tropical North Queensland Best Restaurant three years' running; being included in the prestigious Mietta's Diners Club Australian Restaurant Guide, 2001 and 2002; Craig being included in Mietta's exclusive Great Australian Chefs, 2001; and, as a reflection of his tireless advocacy of Australian cuisine and native ingredients and his close and strong relationship with local suppliers and the wider Cairns community, being inducted into the Tourism Tropical North Queensland Hall of Fame.

Food and Ingredients

Craig proudly flies the flag for modern Australian cuisine and indigenous ingredients, seeking to showcase the best Tropical North Queensland's huge variety of produce in an environmentally sustainable way.

His passion is reflected in Ochre Restaurant's eclectic and engaging menu. His Tempura Bugs from the Gulf of Carpentaria skewered on fragrant Lemongrass, or his Antipasto Plate of Kangaroo Terrine, Crocodile Wonton, Ocean Trout Gravlax and Emu Paté is almost like a landscape painting, featuring the very best local ingredients, including crocodile raised down the road, macadamias grown on local tablelands or cheese from one of Cairns's best dairies all supporting the equally passionate niche growers, farmers and fishermen whose sustainable, organic and small-scale ventures guarantee the very best. Of course, bush tucker is integral to Ochre Restaurant's menu - and singular popularity. Fresh finger limes, lemon aspen, lemon myrtle or bush tomatoes accentuate the truly unique flavour of the region and the cuisine.

The icing on the Wattleseed Pavlova isn't just the amazing taste or fantastic environmental benefits - despite the harshness of the Australian climate and environment, Australian Native Food's are highly nutritious and packed with health benefits. Despite having been ignored for most of European settlement, studies by the Australian Government's Rural Industries Research and Development Corporation (RIRDC) and the industry association Australian Native Food Industry Limited (AMFIL) have revealed thirteen fruits and spices including pepper leaf, quandongs and lemon myrtle, to be "super foods" rich with high concentrations of anti-oxidants, vitamins, minerals and other vital nutrients. Kangaroo meat's ninety-eight percent fat-free!

Salt and Pepperleaf Prawns and Crocodile with Vietnamese Pickles, Lemon Aspen Sambal

serves four as entree

ingredients

Salt and Pepperleaf Prawns and Crocodile
- 16 prawns, peeled and de-veined
- 16 thin slices crocodile
- 1 cup potato flour or corn flour
- 1 tablespoons sesame oil
- 1 garlic clove, finely chopped
- 1 teaspoon sambal oelek
- sea salt
- ground pepperleaf

Vietnamese Pickle Marinade
- 50ml rice wine vinegar
- 1 tablespoons salt
- 2 tablespoons coriander leaves
- 1 teaspoon fresh ginger, chopped finely
- flesh of half a lemon, rind and seeds removed
- 1 bird's eye chilli, with seeds included and finely chopped
- 1 clove garlic, peeled
- 1 teaspoon white sugar

Vietnamese Pickled Vegetables
- 1 bunch bok choy
- ¼ Chinese cabbage
- 1 carrot
- 1 red capsicum
- 1 small daikon radish

Lemon Aspen Sambal
- 2 440g tins tomato purée
- ½ cup vegetable oil
- 1 brown onion
- 1 bunch coriander roots and stalk
- 2 tablespoons tomato paste
- 1 tablespoons sambal oelek
- 2 tablespoons lemon aspen purée
- 4 birds eye small red chilli
- 3 garlic cloves, finely chopped
- 2 tablespoons ginger, grated
- 1 tablespoons palm sugar, grated
- 1 teaspoon blachan

method

Vietnamese Pickles (day before)
Cut all vegetables into thin strips, 8mm wide and 3mm thick. Mix marinade ingredients in food processor until puréed. In a non-reactive bowl, mix vegetables in marinade until thoroughly coated. Store in airtight container in fridge overnight - keeps for 2 weeks.

Lemon Aspen Chilli Sambal (day before, makes approximately 1L)
In food processor, make sambal by puréeing coriander, garlic, ginger, onions and chilli. Wrap blachan in foil and roast on hob until fragrant (about 2 - 3 minutes). Heat vegetable oil in wok, then fry blachan for a few seconds.

Add sambal and remaining ingredients, then simmer gently for an hour, or until mixture thickens. Allow to cool, then blend in food processor. Store in fridge overnight - you're making 1L so you can enjoy spicy delights for the rest of the week, but the Sambal will keep for up to 3 weeks in an airtight container in the fridge.

Salt and Pepperleaf Prawns and Crocodile
Remove Vietnamese Pickles and Lemon Aspen Chilli Sambal from fridge and rest to room temperature. Arrange a bed of Vietnamese Pickles on serving plate.

Cut crocodile into thin slices. Pat prawns and crocodile dry with kitchen paper, then toss in potato flour - if you don't have potato flour, you can use cornflour.

Deep fry flour coated prawns and crocodile in a pot of vegetable oil at 180°C until colour turns golden - about 2 - 3 minutes.

Quickly stir fry sambal oelek and garlic in sesame oil for 30 seconds until sizzling then add prawns and crocodile. While still in the hot fry pan sprinkle over sea salt and ground pepper leaf to taste and toss to mix through.

Serve on bed of Vietnamese Pickles, with small bowls of Lemon Aspen Chilli Sambal on the side. Enjoy with a lively Australian pinot grigio or fragrant semillon sauvignon blanc!

Ochre Restaurant and Catering
43 Shields Street
Cairns, QLD, 4870
Ph: 07 4051 0100
info@ochrerestaurant.com.au
www.ochrerestaurant.com.au

Saffrron Restaurant

Selvam Kandasamy

Born in an idyllic South Indian village outside Madras where 'till this day my father has a small plot of land where he grows rice and grazes buffalo,' Selvam Kandasamy would walk to his grandparents' house after school, helping his beloved grandmother with the cooking. 'It was here I learnt how to make buffalo milk yoghurt,' says Selvam fondly. 'And learnt all about the many spices of South India and how to blend different combinations to achieve aromatic flavours.'

After studying hotel and catering management at the prestigious University of Madras, Selvam's passion for cooking grew and he began to experiment and compile his own recipes, specialising in tandoori, Southern and North Indian cuisines. He was soon snapped up by India's premier hotel, the ITC Park Sheraton, and despite job offers to go to the United States or United Kingdom, he came to Australia, because he wanted the challenge of introducing traditional Indian cuisine to Darwin, which up until he arrived had nothing to offer in this style of cooking.

After working in some of Darwin's best restaurants and hotels, winning some of its top hospitality awards, and writing for local, interstate and international newspapers, Selvam, proudly Australian and happily married to the lovely Joanna, opened Saffrron in 2008.

Featured in magazines such as Australian Table, Australian Gourmet Traveller and Scoop Traveller, books such as Coast Cookbook, and selected as one of Australia's Top 100 Chefs in 2004, Selvam has championed Indian cuisine of the highest standard and freshest ingredients as he has pioneered environmental achievements which have made Saffrron one of Australia's greenest - and spiciest - dining experiences!

How would you describe your cooking style?

Creating healthy, flavourful authentic Indian food people will enjoy. It pleases me very much seeing people enjoying what I've cooked! I've specialised in the three most popular Indian cuisines familiar to people in Australia: traditional tandoori, North and South Indian. Using simple, clean, fresh ingredients, I love coming up with healthy food with intense flavour.

Who's had the most influence over you with the food that you cook?

My family and culture in India, but most importantly my mum Santha, of course!

What do you think makes your Indian style stand out from the rest?

I ensure we use fresh local produce. On Sundays I go to Darwin's Rapid Creek Market where I buy fresh produce from our fabulous local producers. Fresh produce can mean the difference between a mediocre curry or a curry that you'll keep coming back for! I want Saffrron customers to enjoy exceptional tasting curries and actually taste the wonderful flavours that make them so good.

What ingredients are you particularly proud of and encourage others to use?

All the spices, especially chilli, turmeric, coriander and cumin, both seeds and ground. We sometimes call this mix garam masala, and it's the basis of all curry powders. So when you make a curry, you start by browning your onions, then adding your spices, your seeds, curry leaves, whatever meats or veggies you're using, tomatoes and water.

But it all comes back to the spices - stale or pre-processed spices just don't have the same amazing flavour. We buy all our spices fresh and use spices and ingredients people mightn't know about or shy away from at home. Unlike curries from other countries, Indian curries don't use stock, but rather water or coconut milk to cut the chilli heat. If you add stock to an Indian curry it'll just kill the taste of the curry powder. And it depends on the curry, too. When we cook vegetables and vegetable curries, we use mustard seeds, cumin seeds and dried chilli. With meat curries you also add cardamoms, cloves, cinnamon and bay leaves. A lot of chicken and seafood dishes use fenugreek with tamarind or lime juice.

What makes Saffrron so unique?
We aim to combine exquisite Indian cuisine with a new, innovative concept of eco-friendly dining. Saffrron's the first restaurant in the country to achieve Ecotourism's Climate Action Certification, and the first in the Northern Territory to receive Restaurant and Catering Australia's Green Table Certification.

Give us your thoughts on ecological responsibility in the cooking world.
The survival of our business, businesses in general, and ultimately,

the entire human race depends on the survival of our environment.

At Saffrron it's something we feel really strong about and we've got many green mechanisms in place.

What energy saving practices do you use in Saffrron?
We've started implementing procedures and strategies that reduce our carbon footprint and our impact on the environment. We're also proud to be the first restaurant in Australia to use tableware made from begasse, which is derived from sugarcane and is 100% biodegradable and renewable, so it creates much less waste than traditional plastic tableware.

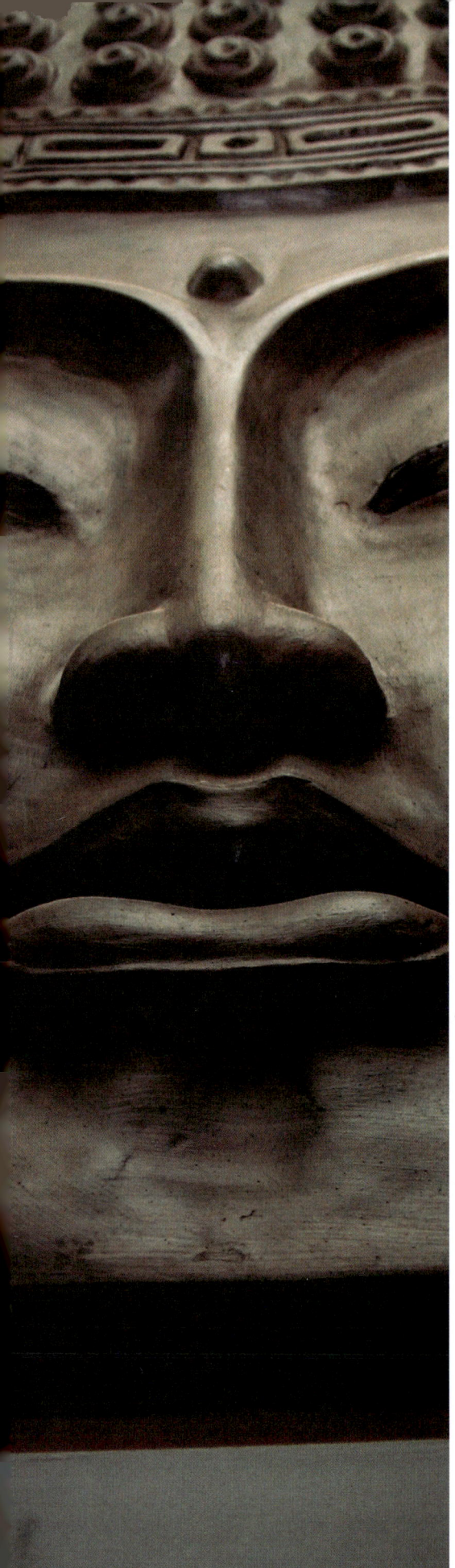

Tell us more about that!

All our sugarcane tableware's manufactured by Eatware (which you can purchase from biodegradable online sites like www.greenwares.com.au, www.biopak.com.au or www.easylivinggreenproducts.com.au). The manufacturing process creates no emissions and because it uses much less energy, it's far friendlier to the environment than manufacturing ceramics. Our biodegradable cutlery's made of cornstarch and our takeaway bags are also biodegradable. In the kitchen, we save waste by only using appropriate stock. Waste cooking oil's sent to Fryer Fuels, which recycles used cooking oil for biodiesel. We even stock Cascade Green beer, because its production is 100% carbon-offset. We minimise our use of plastic where possible and recycle all glass bottles, paper material, tin cans and plastic. We use recycled paper, recycled cartridges, and avoid printing as much as possible with website promotions, e-mail marketing, receiving bills online; and our takeaway menu's printed with soya-based inks on chlorine-free paper that's recycled under the Environmental Management System ISO 14001.

What challenges did you face using this innovative tableware?

At the start, it was a big challenge facing the prejudices of diners who expected to eat off crockery when they ate out. They couldn't make the connection between what we were trying to do, and the disparity between the high standard of the food and what they saw as disposable tableware. I suppose many thought you couldn't be gourmet without fancy crockery! But standing by us through all our ups and downs and little battles have been my parents-in-law, Sue and David Thom. Without their continual love and support through those difficult early days, we mightn't even be here to tell you how much we've achieved.

How have your clientele responded to your great green efforts?

[laughs] You know what? Once they came round, they loved it! Most of them congratulate us on what we're doing and what we're trying to achieve. They're also proud that they're also doing something for the environment by eating at one of Australia's greenest restaurants.

Venue

Vibrant, spicy, exotic and environmentally friendly? Just four kilometres from Darwin City in trendy Parap Village, one of Darwin's funkiest food destinations, Saffrron has quickly established itself as one of the Territory's best restaurants. And its most environmentally friendly, being the first restaurant in the country to achieve Ecotourism's Climate Action Certification, and the first in the Northern Territory to receive Restaurant and Catering Australia's Green Table Certification. It's such commitment to quality with a conscience that have made Saffrron finalists in the PowerWater Melaleuca Environmental Awards for Environmental Advocacy for two years' running and then winning the award this year.

But while Selvam delights in discussing the finer points of water and energy reduction with interested diners, it's not the only reason people keep coming back again and again, so much so that Selvam recommends you book online, especially on weekends, to avoid disappointment. Tasteful hues of deep red chilli, dark mustard brown and yellow turmeric, soft energy efficient lighting and a friendly, casual ambience all add to the welcoming atmosphere, while behind the scenes, Selvam and his staff have reduced chemical cleaning products where possible, using eucalyptus oil and bi-carb soda for much of our cleaning.

In addition to South Indian Sundays, lunch and dinner, Saffrron offers deluxe takeaways and banquets for functions fit for a maharaja, as well as catering and finger foods for any occasion, party - or monsoon weddings!

Food and Ingredients

Saffrron's rich and extensive menu reflects Selvam's influences and experience - from the fragrant delicacies of his idyllic South Indian childhood to the tandoori and North Indian specialties he picked up in his training and career. Enjoy a varied spread from the land, the garden and the ocean, including familiar favourites, exotic new discoveries, and Selvam's own tempting inventions, drawing on his ancient heritage and Darwin's rich fresh produce.

Well-known entrées are given the Saffrron twist with the Calamari Pakora, tender shallow-fried calamari pieces coated with ajwain seeds, coarse rice and chickpea flours; and amidst delicacies from the tandoor like Kastoori Tikka, bite-sized chicken thigh fillets marinated with ginger, garlic, green chillies, lime juice, yoghurt and dry fenugreek leaves; you can discover South Indian delights like 65 Chicken, shallow-fried and marinated with lime juice, ginger and garlic and red chilli powder or the Spinach and Onion Vada, a kind of Indian savoury donut with baby spinach, onion, ginger and curry leaves.

From the land, Selvam offers traditional Indian restaurant standards, including Beef Vindaloo, Lamb Korma and Butter Chicken, as well as South Indian "must-tries" like the spicy and intriguing Pepper Chicken Chettinad, a classic of South India's famous Chettinad cuisine, India's most aromatic; and Malabar Beef Curry, simmered with onion, tomato, aniseed, fennel seed, and coconut milk from the lush shores of Kerala.

From the ocean, Selvam offers Salmon Moli, Tasmanian salmon cubes poached in a mild ginger and turmeric-flavoured coconut curry; and Saffrron's most popular dish, Barramundi Varvul, grilled barramundi marinated with ginger, garlic, lime juice and chilli.

Reflecting many Indians' vegetarianism, Selvam has a cornucopia of herbivorous delights, from a Mixed Vegetable Curry of carrot, broccoli, cauliflower and green peas cooked in a rich and mild cashew curry; Moong Dhal Tadka, green and yellow lentils tempered with garlic, mustard and curry leaves; and more exotic specialties like Bhindi Masala, a rich curry of okra tossed with an onion and tomato-based masala; or Potato Podimass, mashed potato tossed with chickpeas, onions, green chilli, coconut and curry leaves.

In addition to a wide array of Indian breads fresh from the tandoor, there's some interesting sides, including Indian Flag Dips of raita, tomato and mint chutneys reflecting the Indian national colours; and homemade hot pickles made to Selvam's grandmother's secret family recipe. There's a generous selection of mild nibbles for kids and an indulgent spread of rich, perfumed Indian sweets, including Saffrron Kulfi, home-made Indian ice cream flavoured with rosewater, saffron and pistachio; Hot Gulab Jamuns - delicious with ice cream!; and Vatthalappam, a sweet custard of coconut milk, cardamom and egg.

And every Sunday's South Indian Sunday at Saffrron. In addition to the regular menu, customers can choose from a selection of thali banquets such as the Bollywood Thali, Lazy Sunday Thali, Saffrron Special Thali or Express Thali, all with a full Indian meal on a plate for two.

Barramundi Varvul

serves two as a main

'A Madras classic, this always reminds me of home,' says Selvam. 'But I've added a Territory twist with the barra, reflecting the wonderful seafood we have here in Darwin, and that it's my home. And the barra stands up very well to the spices' intense flavours, making this an aromatic - and too easy - seafood treat for two people.'

You can get curry leaves from any good Asian, Sri Lankan, Indian or Fijian grocery store, dried or preferably fresh.

ingredients

1 whole barramundi, about 700g
1 cup fresh lime juice (from 5 limes)
½ cup vegetable oil
½ cup chilli powder
½ cup coriander powder
3 tablespoons fresh ginger, chopped
10 cloves garlic
2 tablespoons turmeric powder
1 bunch fresh coriander leaves, stalks removed (about 1 cup)
2 limes, cut into wedges
4 curry leaves
1 Spanish onion, finely sliced
1 cucumber, finely sliced
salt to taste
pappadums

method

Scale and clean barramundi and pat dry with kitchen paper or towel (or get your fishmonger to do this for you). Make deep gashes in each side of fish.

Chop ginger and garlic and blend to make a fine paste, adding a little water as needed. In a large bowl combine ginger-garlic paste with turmeric, chilli powder, coriander power, lime juice, vegetable oil and salt to make a fine paste without any lumps.

Rub entire barramundi with paste, working it into the gashes, then cover and put in refrigerator to marinate for at least 5 hours.

Before cooking, slice Spanish onion and cucumber finely and cut lime into wedges. Heat 1 tablespoon of vegetable oil in a griddle or frypan to medium hot. Cook fish for 5 minutes, then turn and cook for same time until both sides are golden-brown and fish is cooked.

Garnish with curry leaves, fresh coriander leaves, lime wedges, sliced onion and cucumber.

Serve with steamed basmati rice and pappadums - a great way to make quick, crunchy, fat-free pappadums is to place four or five in the microwave and whizz them until they're brown - about 30 seconds or so. But be careful, they can burn, so keep your eye on them!

And if it's just too spicy for you, add some cool, refreshing yoghurt.

green tips

Ditch the chemicals
How ever did people keep their homes so spick and span before chemicals? With vinegar, bicarbonate of soda and eucalyptus oil, that's how - and that's how Selvam and his team keep Saffrron shining! You don't need lots of potentially harmful chemicals to clean up around the house - use your own homemade alternatives and save your budget and health! For more tips on natural cleaning, check out The Green Pages, Australia's biggest green directory, for tips and products at http://www.thegreenpages.com.au/Green-Eco-Directory/Cleaning.

Steam Clean
Buy a steam mop - you'll save heaps of water and you won't need any chemicals!

Be green beyond the groceries
It's great that so many people are now more aware of things like sustainability, ethicality and food miles. But how many people are aware they can make sure their kitchens can be green too? Turn off appliances at the switch - microwaves use up to 15% of their energy while on standby. Or better yet, put them on timer switches to automatically turn on and off so you don't have to remember! When you use the stove top, heat slowly and use the right burner for the pot - don't use the big burner for a little pot: it won't heat any quicker and wastes needless energy.

Saffrron Restaurant
Shop 14/34 Parap Road
Parap NT 820
Ph: 08 8981 2383
info@saffrron.com
www.saffrron.com

Grumpy's Green

Nick Johnston and Imogen Leaver

What do you get when you mix a moody muso with a vivacious veggo? Grumpy's Green: an eco-friendly inner city lounge bar in Fitzroy where you can "eat, drink, and save the world."

Returning from a nine-year stint working in the bars and restaurants of Paris, Nick Johnston was impressed by the sophistication of the Australian palate, reflected by the number and quality of small brewers in Victoria. Now, his passion's split between organic, locally-brewed artisan beers, and playing blues-rock guitar, with Grumpy's Green offering generous helpings of both. Four nights a week, Nick oversees the bar's live music, including the regular Friday night gig he shares with local muso Andrew Swann.

When she's not frolicking in the park with her beloved puppy Atlas, co-owner Imogen Leaver works her charm behind the bar, as well as looking after Grumpy's Green's admin and advertising.

Grumpy's Green serves up sustainable and locally-brewed beer, wine and food from around Victoria, with a wide range of great food from around the world, including Nepalese, Italian, Mexican, Asian and good old Aussie pub grub. The provenance of everything is researched thoroughly before making it into the cellar or onto the menu.

What makes your establishment unique?
Nick: Our vegetarian pub grub.
Imogen: You can save the world while you eat and drink! A percentage of every sale helps fund a carbon-offset scheme we've set up through Green Fleet to fund a native revegetation program.

How do you save energy?
Imogen: We use energy saving light bulbs and LED lighting, and we turn off all switches, even the fridge lights, when we close up. We're saving up for a solar panel to power as many parts of Grumpy Green's as possible. We specify our "eco-friendliness" when advertising for employment positions and run all staff through "our way" during induction. As a result, everyone's constantly coming up with new suggestions and ways to better our approach. It's part of every decision we make.

What inspired you to embrace a sustainable/local/organic approach?
Imogen: It just makes sense. We try to support local businesses in every way we can, not just for carbon footprint purposes, but to help create a community! We'll be able to source even more locally grown and sustainable produce soon - my mum's just bought three acres of orchards near Castlemaine. She grows everything organically, and we're going to supply her with all our food scraps for compost in return for lovely fresh fruit and vegetables.
Nick: I always enjoyed the regional variety of European food, and I believe it's something that we should embrace here in Oz - our beer list is a prime example of that. As for the carbon offset scheme, we wanted to do something to offset the alcohol miles in the products that we've got in the bar from outside Australia. We had to stock more than just Australian products to attract people to the bar, so we decided to put a percentage of the sales of all drinks, not just the imported ones, into a carbon offset scheme.

How do your customers respond to that?
Nick: I don't think most are aware of it. Anyway, we don't push it. After all, our customers don't come to be lectured, they come to be comfortable and enjoy the atmosphere and the beer.

What are your favourite places to visit for beer and wine?
Imogen: There are some wonderful places in Yarra Valley and the Pyrenees in Western Victoria. I love visiting our Victorian breweries and vineyards to taste the local produce whilst overlooking stunning views. Some of my favourites are Red Hill Brewery and Winery, Beechworth Brewery, Holgate Brewery and Otway Estate Brewery and Winery. Our house beer is Otway's Organic Lager.
Nick: I'd have to say anywhere on the Mediterranean coast. I love their use of local produce. Nothing makes you more creative than having to work with limited ingredients, using just what's around you. In Victoria, I like Goulburn Valley, especially Rees Miller Organic Winery.

How would you best describe your beer and wine styles?
Nick: We specialise in beers - and Victorian ones only at that - much more than we do wines. In fact, I think you could say it's more of a beer bar that serves vegetarian pub grub. We've got everything from lagers and pilseners; wheat and heffeweizen styles; and ales through to stouts. All delicious! Our wine range is small but selective. We stock organic varieties, including shiraz, merlot, pinot noir and pinot grigio.

What are your thoughts on organic food?
Imogen: We're trying to live as clean a life as possible. I think the less we can do with chemicals the better. We try to select organic produce whenever we can, within limitations of cost and availability.

Growing food organically means not putting anything into the soil that doesn't need to be there. It's about sustaining the cycle of nature.

The fact that we serve organic food is a positive for us with some of our customers, who come in expressly for our food.

And, dare I ask, GM food?
Imogen: Mother Nature's a smart woman - don't mess with her!

How important are food miles when you select your produce?
Imogen: Hugely!

We have the kilometres travelled printed on our menus for customers to see.

What ingredients are you particularly fond of and encourage others to use?
Imogen: Our infused vodkas. We're always thinking of new and interesting infusions.
Nick: We get a lovely organic vodka, Vodka O, which we infuse with as many organic flavours we can think of: organic coffee, mandarin, lychee, black cherry, Redskin [lolly], chilli and lime vodkas. We serve our flavoured vodkas straight up, on ice. Stocking organic alcohol's important to us, and when customers realise it's organic, they're usually very happy.

How often do you change your menu?
Imogen: We like to change the menu as the weather changes. I love winter for hearty meals and red wine. In colder months we make soups and cook more curries, including a lovely Nepalese-style curry served on rice with naan bread. And our flourless chocolate cake's a nice dense dessert for winter.

If you had your own food show, what would you call it?
Imogen: Imo's Eco Travels. It'd be a small video camera following me around on my adventures with beer, wine and looking for eco-friendly ideas around the world.
Nick: Eat, Drink and Save The World: how to enjoy yourself and save the planet at the same time.

What's your pet hate about the food industry?
Imogen: It ruins your clothes!
Nick: People. Only joking! Partly.

What's the future got in store for Grumpy's Green?
Imogen: To continue to be a "home away from home" for all our local and regular customers. I've still got great plans to improve it environmentally; I'd love to grow further in the music scene and, obviously, financially. I'd never want it to lose its original essence though.
Nick: We'd love to increase the energy-saving aspect of the bar by using solar power and by capturing more rainfall. Basically, we want to be as independent as possible.

Venue

This eco- and family-friendly beer bar in Fitzroy, where you can

"eat, drink and save the world"

has comfortable couches scattered everywhere. It is like a home away from home… only better! The beautiful beer garden's open seven days a week, and it's a perfect spot to enjoy the sunshine, accompanied by local Victorian beer, organic wine, gluten-free and vegetarian food. Sundays in the courtyard are a great hit with families and groups of friends. For more intimate surroundings, you can enjoy the comfy couches in the cosy main bar.

Grumpy's Green's distinctive vegetarian menu offers a mix of pub favourites, like burgers and nachos, as well as Nepalese, Italian and Asian delicacies. The all-time favourite is the secret recipe veggie Tower Burger - a chickpea patty with lettuce, tomato, carrot, beetroot, alfalfa, mustard mayo and crinkle cut chips. It's closely followed by the mouth-watering Eggplant Parma on a bed of rocket, topped with capsicum, cheese and Napoli sauce and a bed of home made chips. Other faves are beer battered eggplant wedges with tomato chutney; spicy chickpea tortillas with cheese avocado and sour cream; and chickpea tempura vegetables with house-made dipping sauce. If you're coeliac and craving a pizza, Tuesday night is $7 Pizza Night, with gluten-free pizza available. You can even wash it down with a gluten-free beer or three!

With their huge selection of Victorian microbrewery beers, wines and local spirits, you'll soon discover just how enjoyable saving the planet can be. Rock-blues guitarist Nick oversees live music gigs every Thursday, Friday and Saturday from 9pm.

Though it's probably the first bar in Australia committed to becoming carbon neutral, Grumpy's Green's eco-friendliness isn't obvious. And that's the way Nick and Imogen like it - they've taken care of the "saving the world" part so you can get on with the eating and drinking!

Food and Ingredients

Victorian beers and wines are the stars at Grumpy's Green. However, as Imogen says, 'We started providing food because people were asking for nibbles with their drinks. We already had a huge kitchen, so we hired a chef to produce sustainable food and to show that it's not that hard to make choices that have a positive effect on the environment.' Carbon miles for every beer, wine or menu item are printed for everyone to see.

Grumpy's Green's range of beers is staggering: six different lagers, pilseners and ales on tap, with two additional rotating, seasonal taps; plus another fifty bottled varieties, including porters, stouts and gluten-free ale and pilsener. Wine's also locally-sourced and organic where possible, with a good selection from boutique wineries such as Red Hill Estate on the Mornington Peninsula and the Yarra Valley's first vineyard, the family-owned Kellybrook Estate.

As with their approach to beers and wines, Grumpy's Green's food is local and organic where ever possible. Nick says it's the "great veggo pub grub" that keeps punters coming back and making them locals. Grumpy's Green offers a rich and wide variety, with Asian, Italian and Mexican flavours adding zing and sparkle to fresh, organic, locally-sourced ingredients. Naturally, there's gluten-free and vegan options as well. Everything's made fresh on the premises, even the specially-crinkle cut chips!

Underpinning all this wonderful 21st Century pub grub are the usual suspects: chickpeas and lentils. But good and wholesome doesn't need to mean boring, as Grumpy's Green's exciting and ever-changing menu shows. From bar food including Vego Nachos with Grumpys Own Chilli Bean Sauce, Tasty and Mozzarella Cheese, Sour Cream and Guacamole; tempting tapas-style snacks like Beer Battered Eggplant Wedges with Tomato Chutney, Pumpkin Skewers with Housemade Satay Sauce and Jasmine Rice and Moroccan Spiced Warm Crumbed Olives with Tomato Relish; generous sharing plates, like the Asian Plate with dim sum, samosas, spring rolls and rice paper rolls or the Mezze with marinated mushrooms, egg torta, dip, fetta, stuffed pepperets and crusty toasted bread; and mains like the Tower Burger, a tender housemade veggie pattie with salad, mustard mayo and those handcut chips; Grumpy's Green's ever-popular Summer Wrap, with smoked tofu and lettuce; or the delectable Chickpea and Red Lentil Dhal, whatever you choose at Grumpy's Green, you know it isn't just good for you and the planet, it's delicious too!

Grumpy's Green Nepalese Chickpea and Red Lentil Dhal

serves four as a main

Fresh ginger, garlic, tomatoes, dried and seed spices turn this simple dhal into a mouth-watering dish, equally suitable for winter or summer.

ingredients

1L water
500g red lentils
500g chickpeas
300ml vegetable oil
4 tomatoes, finely diced
1 onion, finely chopped
2 tablespoons cumin
2 tablespoons salt
1 tablespoon fresh coriander, chopped
1 tablespoon garam marsala
1 tablespoon curry powder
½ tablespoon chilli powder
½ tablespoon turmeric powder
½ tablespoon fresh ginger
½ tablespoon fresh garlic
pinch cumin seeds
pinch fenugreek seeds
pinch mustard seeds
2 curry leaves

method

Cover lentils with water. Bring to boil, lower heat and cook for 7 - 8 minutes.

While lentils are cooking, roughly blend chickpeas in a mixer until a similar size to lentils. Add lentils and mix well.

To make dhal base, heat oil in a wok on low heat, then add cumin seeds, fenugreek seeds, curry leaves and mustard seeds and fry gently. Add onion and fry until softens, then add all remaining spices and cook gently. Stir mixture to prevent it burning, then add diced tomatoes and cook through. Keep on low heat and continue stirring until spices are infused.

When base is ready, add chickpea and lentil mix and stir continuously until all ingredients are blended. The dhal is now ready!

Serve with steamed, fragrant jasmine rice or oven-fresh naan bread.

green tips

Educate yourself
There's plenty of information out there to help you make better choices.

Don't forget the little things
It's all the little things that add up, so walk or ride instead of driving and only use or buy what you need - waste not, want not! Repair large household items instead of buying new ones and put on a jumper instead of turning on the heater.

Stay local and plant a tree
Eat local, drink local and plant a few native trees.

Grumpy's Green
125 Smith Street, Fitzroy, VIC 3065
Ph: 03 9416 1944
imogen@grumpysgreen.com
www.grumpysgreen.com

Spice Island

Paul Stafford

Spice Island's Paul Stafford loves islands! After starting out at sixteen making fish and chips at the Onchan Chippy, on the Isle of Man off England's west coast, he completed an Advanced Diploma in Hotel Catering and Management before establishing restaurants such as The Thatched Barn in North Devon's Croyde Bay, which, as one of the United Kingdom's only surfing breaks, is popular with Aussies; and Muswell's in Baker Street in London, where regulars could include British music legends like Paul Weller or Holly Johnson from Frankie Goes to Hollywood. At 25, he followed his itchy feet and burgeoning career to the world's biggest island, Australia, where he met his wife Rachel. Running one of Melbourne's busiest boutique catering companies, Crave Catering, Paul's perspective changed after the birth of their first son, Max.

Looking for the community and relaxed pace offered by Phillip Island, 120 kilometres south-east of Melbourne, Rachel and Paul followed their dreams and established Spice Island, offering an array of green food experiences for visitors and locals alike, from luxurious bed and breakfast studios on Phillip Island; catering for any function or dining experience from ten to a thousand diners; one of Australia's most innovative and exciting cooking schools at San Remo; and the recent acquisition of Spice Island at the Churchill Island Café on beautiful nearby Churchill Island, offering spectacular views of the dramatic Westernport Bay amidst a bucolic setting filled with historic buildings, an ark of friendly animals including Clydesdales, highland cattle, inquisitive sheep, ducks, chickens and a peacock or two! And Paul and Rachel's own one-acre veggie patch, from which they source nearly all their vegetables and herbs for the Café and Cooking School.

From the Isle of Man to here, one small island to another - what attracted you to Phillip Island?

[laughs] We actually had a holiday house here. I had a successful catering company in Melbourne, but when my son Max was born, I had to cater a 750 head function after being with Rachel through a twenty-four hour labour! And I thought to myself, There's got to be a bit more to life than this, especially after Max's birth.

It just so happened everything came together: someone made an offer on the catering company and we decided to make the move down to Phillip Island to live in our holiday house. Originally, we weren't planning to do anything, but being the people we are, we ended up buying a plot of land just before we flew to the UK for a holiday. When we got back we built the Spice Island bed and breakfast and from there it all just evolved.

How important is sustainability?

Vital! I think it's becoming one of the key drivers of a successful business. I think people are really cottoning on to sustainable green living - not just as an idea, but a conscious lifestyle choice. For instance, we use garlic that only comes from down the road, and when people ask me why I buy that garlic, I cut a bulb in half and show them that crunchy and sweet it is. I know Nicole who grows it, and so I know how much work she's put into making it organic and safe, and people love that provenance and assurance. In our cooking classes, we try to use local, seasonal, sustainable, organic green food and produce and explain to people why it's best to use it.

What about food miles?

Food was never meant to travel the way or distances we move it today. The concept of filling in seasonal blanks by moving food across hemispheres is just crazy. Food's heavy and the carbon emissions produced by moving food are simply unsustainable and unacceptable.

Are these ideas of self-sustainability and locality important to your cooking school?

Absolutely! It's interesting, you know: I find it a lot easier teaching the kids that come in than some of the adults. Obviously, a lot of my students are already interested in food, and many buy from the best butchers, the best greengrocers, the best delis and provedores. They demand the best produce, which is great, but often that's at the expense of the green food they could and should be choosing.

Of course, it's fabulous people are more interested in food and food culture, but that interest should be complemented by knowledge and thoughtfulness about how it's produced and where it's come from. It's symptomatic, I guess, of Western culture as a whole, where affluence hasn't made us eat any better - if you look at America, you'd say the opposite!

A lot of people buy something because they're told it's "the best," but surely the best way of determining that isn't because someone else told you so, but because you know the producer, you've seen where it's come from and how it's produced - something you can only really do when you do buy locally and develop relationships with your butcher, grocer, farmer or grower. And it's only really then, when you've become more closely involved in sourcing your food - whether by growing it yourself or by getting to know your suppliers by buying locally - that your interest becomes real knowledge.

What's your opinion of celebrity chefs?

Considering how ignorant people were about good food and cooking when I was growing up, the rise of anything that makes people think about what they eat and how to cook it can only be a good thing, right? Even if often the "quick" dish you see on telly has had an army of producers, stylists and technicians making sure it all comes off on camera, if people are inspired by and want to emulate their

role models - cooking for themselves if they've never done it before or cooking a dish or cuisine they've never tried before - and especially understanding and appreciating good food, ingredients and cooking together with their family, then that's wonderful.

A celebrity chef reaching out to millions of people like, say Jamie Oliver, to eat better and together as a family, is fantastic, and it's something dear to my heart and my family's way of life.

As long as the chef part is given as much air time as the celebrity bit [laughs]...

You grow many of your own vegetables, don't you?
Yeah, we do! We've got an acre of veggie patch over on nearby Churchill Island, which required an enormous effort from Rachel, but it's all running beautifully now, thanks to her. We've had problems with everything from purple hens taking a shine to the tomatoes, to visitors leaving the gates open to allow the sheep in for a free feed! We grow nearly all of our own vegetables - we've got lots of pumpkins at the moment, fabulous silverbeet, an abundance of zucchini and basil, which gets your digestive and creative juices really going! We also preserve lemons from the orchard for our Moroccan cooking class,

and one of our favourite times of the year is when the old hundred year old fig starts to fruit...

You're as committed to the environment as you are to your community. What ideas do you have for contributing more to both?
Well, for the upcoming season, we really want to start putting the spokes on the wheel, so to speak - we've been talking about forming some sort of informal co-operative. We're really lucky to be part of such a wonderful and welcoming community and a lot of people who come into the café and pantry grow their own produce themselves. We'd like the café to not just be a social hub but a place where people can come in and exchange their excess produce and exchange it for other goods or produce.

Venue

It all started with the boutique Spice Island bed and breakfast retreat. With spectacular views of rustic wilderness and wild unspoiled coastline looking out to Bass Strait. Every studio's got king-sized beds, spa, large open plan living areas, luxury Egyptian cotton linen and all the mod-cons. You can have a full 'tapas style' breakfast in bed with eggs from Paul and Rachel's chooks, or else take in Philip and Churchill Islands' beautiful scenery and enjoy it at Spice Island's Cafe at Churchill Island. In addition, there's a range of picnic and indulgence packages to add a little extra romance to your getaway, featuring fully-stocked homemade picnic hampers, passes to all of the Islands' parks, champagne, candles, flowers and chocolate.

The new hub of Spice Island and Churchill Island is Spice Island's Cafe at Churchill Island, set on one of Gippsland's most stunning places, the beautiful and historic Churchill Island, where you can enjoy spectacular views across Westernport Bay while enjoying Paul's gourmet delights. A fabulous venue for events, especially weddings, which can either be catered from the café or stunning marquees. With historic, heritage buildings, a working farm and breathtaking walking tracks, Churchill Island offers a tranquil opportunity to leave the troubles of the world far away on the mainland. And if you listen carefully, you may yet catch a sense of the presence of Indigenous Bunurong people, long departed from these beautiful Islands.

Food and Ingredients

Lovingly grown and conscientiously sourced, Spice Island's green food is of the highest standard. 'I like keeping it simple,' says Paul, 'so that the ingredients can really shine. Funnily enough, the less I do, the better it tastes!' Using only the best local, sustainable, seasonal and ethical green food ingredients where possible, Paul also insists that anything not locally sourced comes from within a 200 kilometre radius and is as organic as possible, like free-range and organic bacon from Melbourne's Belmore Meats, or Nicole's garlic, only a thirty minute drive through the hills in Drouin.

There's the usual brekkie favourites, but what other café could boast the basil and tomatoes had been picked by the chef himself? That freshness shines through in every dish, especially the popular Baked Eggs, Chorizo, Goat's Cheese, Tomato and Basil Pide; or his signature dish, Home Corned Corn Beef Hash with Fried Eggs and HP Sauce (of course).

Lunch brings even more green food delights, reflecting Paul's passion for sustainability and locality. The light and zesty Vine Tomato, Buffalo Mozzarella, Spinach and Basil Pide sings with freshness and flavour; and the Best Tuna Salad with Crisp Shallots, Bean Shoots, Red Onion, Chilli and Lime Dressing lives up to its name, the rich meatiness of the sustainably caught tuna balanced by the spicy and sour contrasts of the dressing and crunchy shallots. With a select wine list of locally produced wines such as Purple Hen and Silverwater the Spice Island Cafe at Churchill Island is a place to linger...

If you'd like to take a little Spice Island home with you, there's a well-stocked Pantry and Café at the new Cooking School in San Remo, offering the best and most sustainable, local and ethical green food delights you can think of, including locally sourced range of preserves and condiments, coatings and ingredients, including native spices and rubs for meat dishes, chutneys and preserves for those gourmet barbecuers who just have to go the extra mile. The pantry also stocks a range of those difficult to source ingredients and a very select range of kitchen utensils.

Or, call on Paul to cater for your next dinner, party or function. Taking the time to tailor the menu to meet your event's exact needs, Paul welcomes you to come and taste an array of potential dishes and options. 'If you visualise it, we can make it happen,' says Paul. From a dinner to impress for eighteen featuring irresistible entrées like Autumn Mushrooms, Asparagus, Fromage Blanc and Thyme and a main course featuring Slow-Roasted Glenloth Corn-Fed Chicken with Braised Tomatoes, Broccolini, Cos, Cucumber and Waxy Potatoes straight from the garden; to a staggering and mouth-watering selection of Paul's favourite finger and bowl foods, including Gippsland Beef with Egg Yolk Soldiers and Shiso Leaf; Mini Chorizo-Style Hotdogs with Aïoli; Slow-Roasted Lamb with Streaky Bacon, Smashed Peas and Reggiano and more - you can relax and let your guests and you enjoy yourselves, knowing not only the service is of the highest standard, but the produce is too.

At the San Remo Pantry Cafe and Cooking School, learn to make anything in four easy and fun hours, from Provincial French, Spanish Tapas and Paella to Fragrant Thai, Japanese and Moroccan classics - with produce straight from the garden, a few drinks and transfers to and from the Island at minimal cost, all learning from one of the warmest, funniest and most passionate teachers you'll ever have!

Dukkah and Crispy Thrice-Cooked Quail
serves six as an entrée or canapé

'Dukkah's one of my favourite ingredients to use,' says Paul. 'Fabulous for canapés and great for tapas - I believe the all best dishes to share with friends involve drinks and fingers, lots of each! My bush tucker-inspired dukkah is great on scrambled eggs, or simply in a bowl with some good quality extra virgin olive oil and grilled sourdough bread for dipping.'

Wattleseeds are prized for their high nutritional content and low glycemic index, making them a great food for diabetics and dieters. Their chocolatey, coffee, hazelnutty flavours make them a great match for the nuts in Paul's Dukkah, with mountain pepper and lemon myrtle giving it a spicy, zesty zing.

You can get wattle seeds, mountain pepper and lemon myrtle from any good healthfood shop, specialty spice shop or provedore, or from Outback Pride (www.outbackpride.com.au) which also gives you information on where to get it. 'Dannic garlic isn't some exotic variety,' Paul laughs. 'It's just what Danni and Nicole who grow it call it!'

ingredients

Dukkah
¾ cup hazelnuts or pistachios
½ cup sesame seeds
2 tablespoons coriander seeds
2 tablespoons cumin seeds
2 tablespoons wattleseeds
4 leaves mountain pepper

Crispy Thrice-Cooked Quail
6 quails
2 tablespoons Dukkah
2 cloves Dannic garlic
1 thumb sized knob ginger
2 lemon myrtle leaves
1 tablespoon honey
1 tbsp extra virgin olive oil

method

Dukkah
Preheat oven to 175°C. Place nuts on baking tray lined with baking paper and bake for about 5 minutes, or until fragrant. While nuts are still hot, pour them onto tea towel. Fold towel over them to cover, then rub vigorously to remove skins. Set aside to cool.

In a dry skillet over medium heat, toast sesame and wattle seeds until light golden brown, about 1 minute. Keep an eye on them and shake or stir them constantly, as they can burn easily at any heat. Pour into a medium bowl as soon as they're done so they won't continue toasting.

In same skillet, toast coriander and cumin seeds while shaking pan until they begin to pop. Pound nuts, seeds and spices coarsely in a mortar and pestle (this can also be done in a spice grinder so long as it's set on a coarse setting) with mountain pepper leaves and store in an airtight container in the pantry. Dukkah should last for 3 - 4 weeks.

Quail
Preheat oven to 180°C. Bone out quail, or get your butcher to do this for you.

Pound garlic, ginger, lemon myrtle leaves and honey in a mortar and pestle. Press paste into flesh side of quail - not skin side. Heat olive oil in fry pan or wok until hot then fry quails skin side down, being careful not to lose too much paste. Fry for 2 - 3 minutes until skin is crisp. Turn and fry other side for 1 minute.

Place quail in ovenproof pan or baking dish and cook for 5 minutes at 180°C.
Remove from oven and finish on hot char grill or barbecue for 2 minutes. Don't worry if there's lots of smoke - it'll only be adding even more flavour! But make sure you cook in a well-ventilated place or open your windows and doors to prevent the fire alarm going off!

Pile high on serving platters and generously drizzle with extra virgin olive oil and good quality salt flakes.
Serve immediately with cold beer, eager fingers - and a fingerbowl!

Spice Island
1A Hill Street
Sunderland Bay VIC 3922
Ph: 03 5956 7557
info@spiceisland.com.au
www.spiceisland.com.au

Stefano's Café Bakery
Stefano di Pieri

Born in the beautiful medieval town of Treviso, near Venice, well-known and much-loved celebrity chef Stefano di Pieri came to Australia in 1974. After studying politics and, of course, Italian studies at Melbourne University, he had a varied career, editing the Italian-language newspaper Nuovo Paese and working in the Victorian Public Service, before eventually settling on the calling that made him famous. Although he trained professionally for a little while, his enthusiasm drove him onto self-taught discoveries - and green food excellence! Drawing on his family's roots as subsistence farmers back in Italy, Stefano's affinity for the land and passion for regional produce brought him, his lovely wife Donata and their family to Mildura, the "Outback Mediterranean" where he soon established himself as a local legend, and their many business ventures, including the highly-acclaimed Stefano's and the Mildura Grand Hotel, as local landmarks. His reputation established by his wonderful ABC TV series, A Gondola on the Murray, it was sealed by his recent Lifestyle Channel series, Stefano's Cooking Paradiso, featuring the same ebullient warmth and great recipes that have made him and his restaurants so deservedly famous!

What are some of Mildura's best kept secrets?
Well, I'd have to say my new Café Bakery! [laughs] And definitely one of the most amazing things is the locally produced Murray River pink salt. Duncan and Jan Thomson intercept brine from the Murray River, producing a beautiful pink salt that's very high in natural magnesium.

And you had something to do with that didn't you?
Ah, a bit! [laughs]. I remember saying to Duncan, 'Look how much these imported English salt flakes are. If you could do the same to all the salt produced by salinity in the Murray River, you could make a fortune!' It was just lying around, and of course, salinity is a huge environmental problem, especially in a country as dry as Australia, and particularly for us in Mildura, who live on and with this great river. From that small idea, the business just took off, and it means that we can enjoy a wonderful, unique product that helps the environment not just by reducing food miles, but by reducing salinity. It's a very romantic and innovative solution to a very big problem.

So what do you use the salt for?
Everything - on the table, in my cooking, even in my in-house baked bread! But it has more flavour than just saltiness - the lovely salmon-pink colour of the salt comes from the minerals and elements such as magnesium and calcium in the brine, giving it a beautiful mellow flavour. There's also a local salt bush, the samphire bush, which draws up salt from the soil as it grows. You may have heard, for example, of saltbush lamb, the deliciously tender lamb that feeds on it. I love it with Murray cod: I blanch it then put it on the fish - it tastes divine! And if you're ever camping around here and find a good fresh samphire bush, you can chuck in your salad!

So the Murray River has a hugely political past. How much water should flow and how much should be used for irrigation. Does this effect you?
Mildura was established by an Act of parliament. And there was a contract between the government and the first irrigators who owned a block of land. And this contract has been ignored by successive governments. It said that they had the right to water, all the way from the river to the farm. If water cuts have to happen, they should stop more growth as opposed to punishing the original farms. We have to cherish the historical industries.

But this was from when the food was produced for Australians. Now a lot of it is for export. Should they get the same resources?
It's appalling that Australian water is on the free market, and at such ludicrously low prices. You can buy Australian water from Singapore or England - what are the environmental costs in that? It's almost criminal. Australian water should belong to the Australian people, Australian producers, Australian farmers - and most importantly, to the fragile Australian environment.

What do you think about bottled water?
Madness! I mean, I think it's good people are starting to question what they're doing, and it's fantastic towns (like Bundanoon in NSW's Southern Highlands) or schools (like North Sydney's Monte Sant'Angelo Mercy College) are banning bottled water. I mean, I remember drinking water out of the tap or bubbler, and studies have shown tap water can actually be less harmful than bottled water - so why drink bottled water just because Coca-Cola tells us to?

From cooking to brewing, you've recently started baking. How did that become a passion?
Well, how couldn't it have? Mildura's surrounded by hundreds of thousands of square kilometres of wheat - we're in the middle of Australia's "wheat belt," which stretches from Broken Hill in NSW all the way down to Bendigo in Victoria. There's beautiful golden wheat everywhere, and what do people eat? Those horrible, thin, cheap, tasteless white frisbees. And because the art of baking has died out, that's what most people think bread is. There are fewer and fewer real bakers who know how to make good, nutritious, delicious bread without chemicals and additives and other artificial ingredients, and yet, if you make bread properly, with passion, you don't need any of that.

It seems ironic that Australia's bread basket should have so few bakeries...
I know, I know… it's the bane of my life! Seeing that lack of traditional bakeries was terribly sad, and I mean that from the heart. So that's why I got Paul, my master baker, who's more important than anyone in terms of what we do, what we're trying to do, to start teaching little kids how to make real bread the traditional way - our own little green food generation!

We should be proud of our produce in the wheat belt - not simply as a commercial export, but a way of life. We should showcase and celebrate the amazing bread we can produce with such wonderful wheat. We should be sharing this with the country and the world!

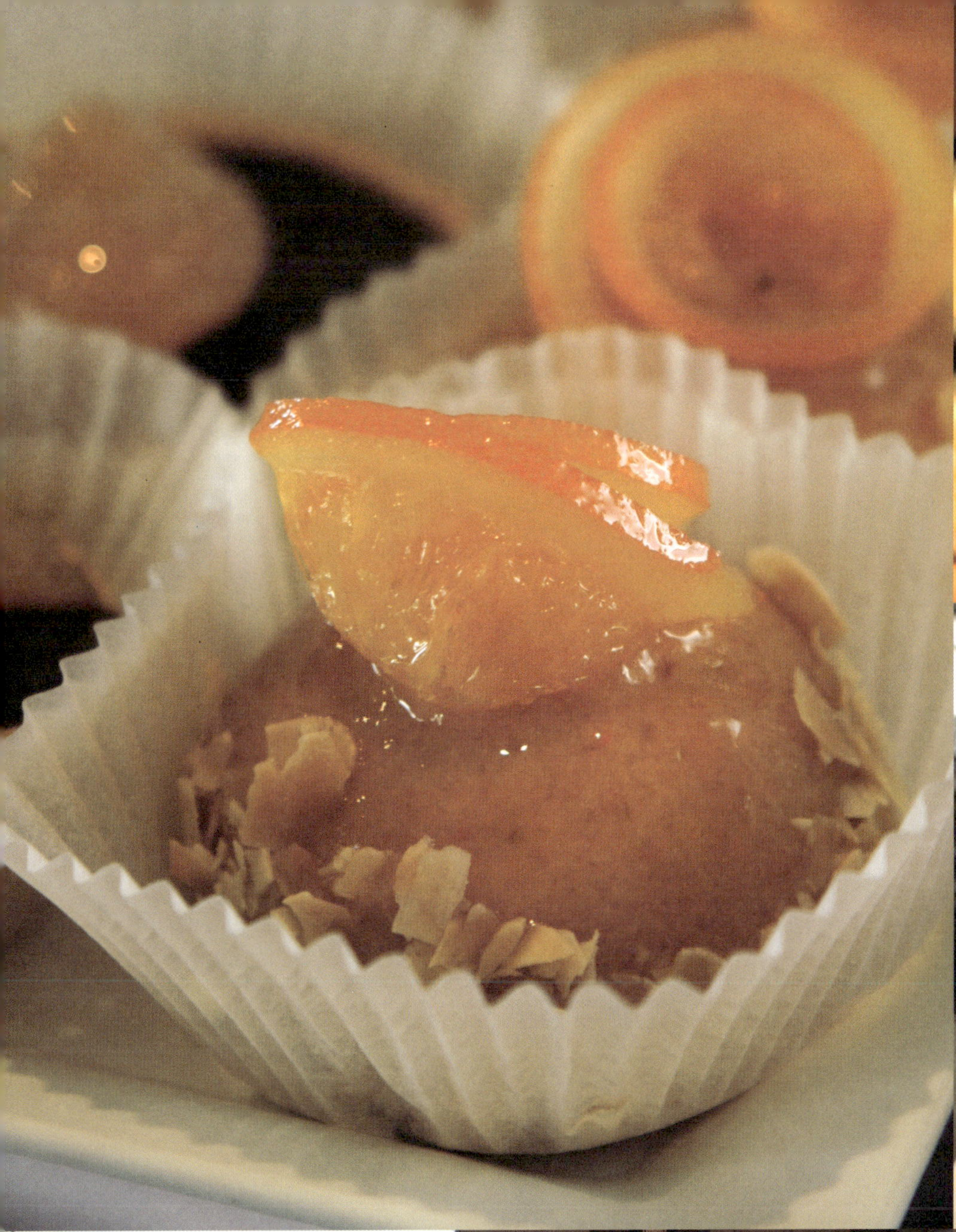

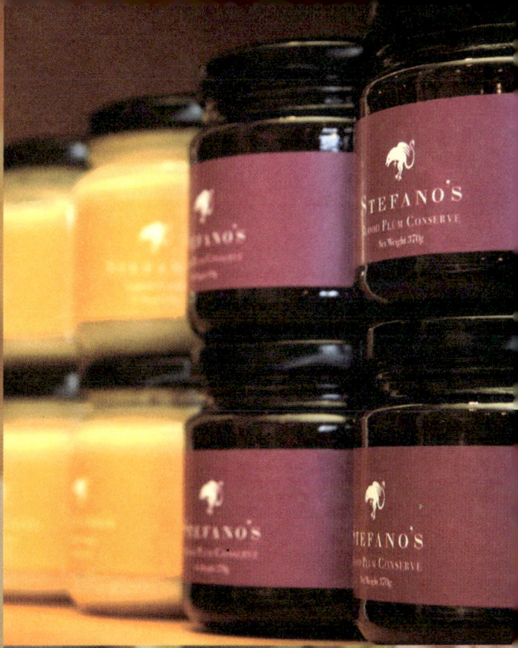
STEFANO'S
PLUM CONSERVE

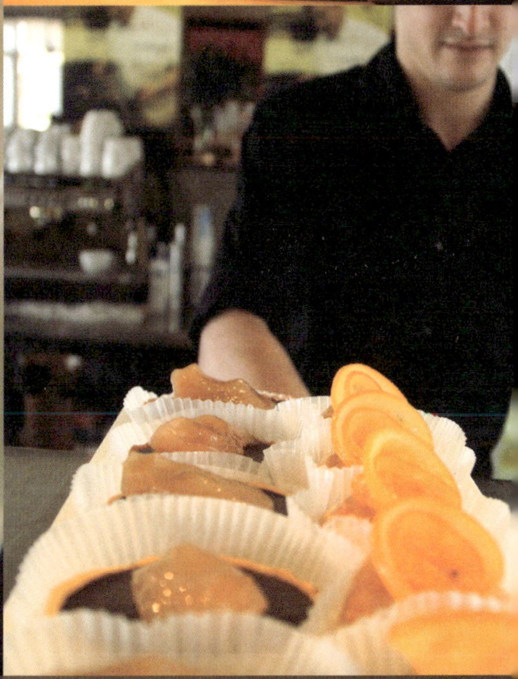

STEFANO'S
CELLAR DOOR & BAR
Mildura Writers Festival
@ Stefano's
Philip Hodgins Memorial Dinner
Friday 16th
Exhibition Opening "Between Worlds"
Wednesday 14th
The Cook And The Cook
Stefano de Pieri And Maggie Beer
aturday Festival Dinner

MILDURA BREWERY
MURRAY
HONEY WHEAT
FINE BREWING

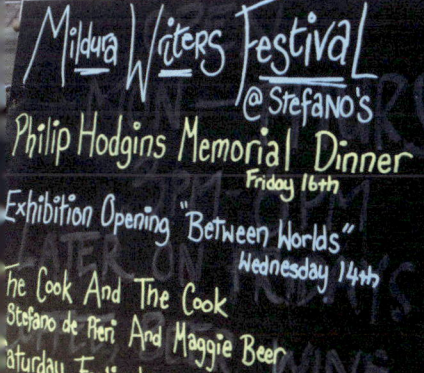

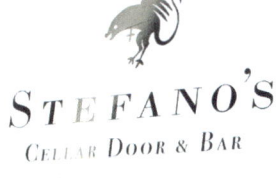

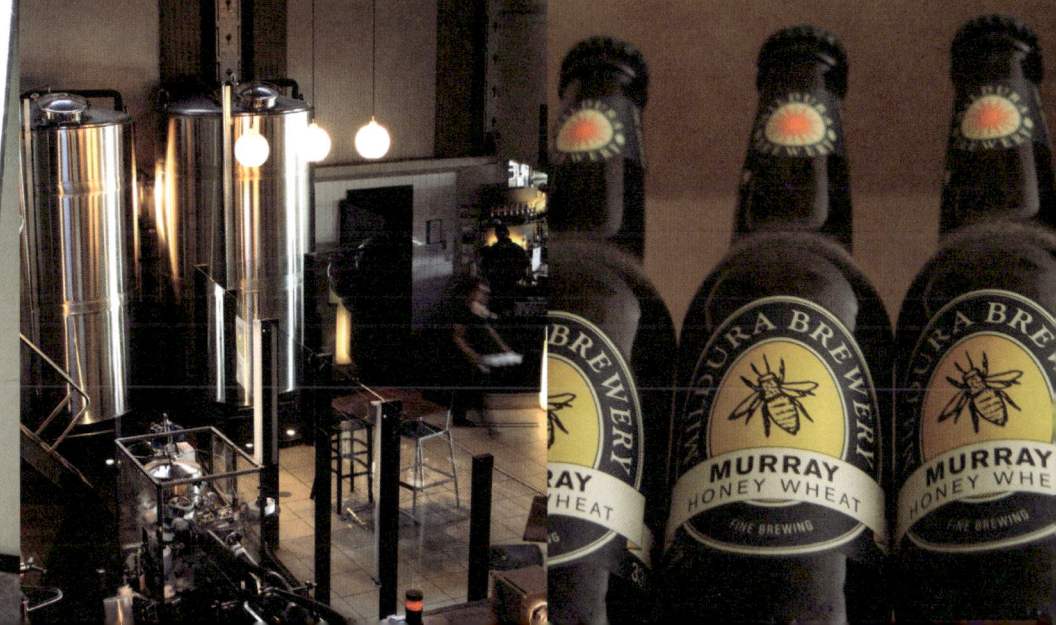

How did people respond to this "new" old bread?
You know what? Let me tell you - when we first started the bakery, I went broke because everybody was so used to buying white sliced bread. I'm not joking - I went completely broke. Thank goodness my restaurant Stefano's could support the loss. It's taken us two goes to make it viable - but now everybody loves it!

What are some of the challenges of using local food?
Like green food, people can be resistant to new food. When I used to do risotto twenty years ago, people would complain 'What is this? It's like rice glug! It took time and persistence, but of course now, it's one of my most popular dishes. It's the same with trying to source locally. Because of our location and given how great the distances are, I have to consider that even local ingredients like yabbies may come from 300 kilometres away, which means a 600 kilometre round trip for the driver. And because my customers love seafood, it has to be on the menu, but it's got to come all the way from Melbourne, nearly 500 kilometres away.

Given my love of the Mildura region, and how much I celebrate its wide variety of produce in my shows, books and restaurants, I do try as hard as I can to keep the menu as seasonal and local as possible, trying to offer seasonal, local alternatives to the other not-so-seasonal, not-so-local options. For example, I've been serving that beautiful, hearty, Northern Italian classic, pasta e fagioli. It's real comfort food, so loved by Italians in cold, lean winters, when other ingredients, more available in other seasons, couldn't be found. Of course, some people will say it's just pasta and beans, but I hope, with the same patience and persistence, they'll love it just as they love risotto now. It's funny - like the bakery,

the real challenges to spreading the green food mantra isn't so much logistical or even economical, it's emotional: getting people to overcome their resistance and try new things.

What do you think best represents Australian cuisine?
Actually, I was in a Melbourne pub the other day, and enjoyed a wonderful lamb and mint pasta. I thought this should be Australia's national dish! It represented Australia's long history of wheat growing and lamb raising, along with immigrant cuisine like pasta, dressed with English culinary traditions like mint sauce. Imaginative, innovative and delicious!

You've achieved so much: spectacularly popular television series, the largest food and drinks empire in Mildura, if not Australia - a café, restaurant, brewery, bakery. Any plans to make candlesticks? When will it all stop?
[laughs] It's stopping right here, right now! As Donata keeps reminding me, I'm not getting any younger, and I want all my extended family and wonderful staff to get a share of the success they've all worked so hard to help contribute to, so I'm slowly divesting myself and taking a back seat - it's their turn now. But, you know, I do still have a few things up my sleeves…

Like what?
The brewery's been an amazing success, and I'd like to expand it so it can continue to keep up with ever growing demand. And before too long, I'd love to do something for the Indigenous people around here, to help drive Indigenous employment and development. I'd always enjoyed working with the Indigenous community, especially taking on Indigenous apprentices - they're great. I'd really like to do something productive with the many talented Indigenous kids I know before I get too much older!

Venue

Where else would a passionate Italian like Stefano settle, but Mildura, "the Outback Mediterranean?" At once undeniably Aussie, surrounded by magnificent bushland, breathtaking salt pans, the mighty Murray River and magnificent wheat fields for as far as the eye can see, it's also a vibrant multicultural community, thanks to energetic immigrants like Stefano, abundant with vineyards, citrus and olive groves, celebrating the good things of life: family, friends, good food and drink.

And nobody loves these things more than Stefano! Starting with the refurbishment of the majestic Mildura Grand Hotel in 1991, he's made immense contributions to every facet of Mildura life: from his much-loved and much-lauded restaurant, Stefano's, which has won countless awards, including Australian Gourmet Traveller's Restaurant of the Year Award and two coveted Chef's Hats in The Age Good Food Guide; to the popular Stefano's Cellar Door and Bar, which showcases his much-awarded range of Stefano di Pieri wines and Mildura Brewery beers, naturally brewed on premises. Don't forget to check out the beautiful Gallery 25 Artist's Space, or his newest passion, the Café Bakery, where you can enjoy some of the fruits of his and Paul's labours.

Whether you want to enjoy a few drinks at the Cellar Door and Bar, appreciate art at Gallery 25, enjoy a casual lunch or pick up some real bread from the Café Bakery, or enjoy a more sophisticated meal at Stefano's, there's something for everyone. And you can keep enjoying Stefano's incomparable hospitality by staying a few nights at the Mildura Grand Hotel!

Food and Ingredients

At the Café Bakery, the new hub between the Cellar Door and Bar and Gallery 25, how will you decide between such a stunning assortment of Italian, Continental and Australian bakery and patisserie favourites, including moist foccacia; sweet and savoury croissants; breathtaking flans and tarts; cakes; biscuits; Paul's signature custard "bombe;" and what Stefano reckons is 'the best vanilla slice in the Mallee!'

At brekkie, you can enjoy a familiar cast of favourites like local, organic, free-range eggs cooked any way you like, served with local smoked bacon and Stefano's gourmet tomato relish. For lunch, why not try Stefano's home-made Cannelloni with Spinach and Ricotta, Pasta with Meat Balls or the now popular Mushroom Risotto?

Why not relax with a glass of Stefano's Tre Viti, a light red wine 'unlike any other in Australia?' says Stefano. 'It's very balanced and quaffable, with subtle cherry flavours and very mild tannin. In Italy, we sometimes drink it before noon - go on, indulge yourself!' Another popular choice is Stefano's Arneis, a fresh Piedmontese white, more like a lighter pinot grigio with subtle summer fruits and light aromatics.

You can also sample some of the Mildura Brewery's prize-winning beers and ales. Try the Mallee Bull, a full-bodied and powerful ale with great flavour and length, brewed with Carapils, chocolate and roast malt; or, given Stefano's celebration of the wheat belt, the cleansing and delectable Murray Honey Wheat Beer. And, for the recipe he generously shares with us, Stefano says 'you have to have my own Pilsner, a crisp sessional brew with a long-lasting palate, ideal for the richness of my Yabbies and Sausage Scrambled Eggs!'

Yabbies and Sausage Scrambled Eggs

serves two

This is what I'd call A Country Breakfast - with beer! I remember travelling in Malaysia and loving how they fearlessly combined ingredients. They just used everything: pork, fish, vegetables, eggs, noodles… and I thought why don't we do that here? This is a delicious and easy breakfast that can be served with fresh bread… and a lovely cold beer, like Stefano's own Pilsner. Saluté!

ingredients

6 freshwater yabbies, cooked (prawns can be used if you can't get yabbies)
6 eggs
2 large Italian sausages
1 pinch Murray River salt
1 small drizzle of garlic oil
fresh crushed black pepper
butter

method

Marinate yabbies with garlic oil and salt for 20 minutes. Of course, Stefano recommends his premium garlic oil, but if you can't get it, get the best extra virgin olive oil you can find and throw three roughly crushed garlic cloves into the bottle and let it infuse for about two days.

Whisk eggs lightly, then reserve.

Remove sausage mince from casings, then separate into little lumps with butter in hot fry pan for 5 minutes, or until brown. Throw in yabbies and eggs.

Be quick to fold everything together so they don't go rubbery! Don't forget the yabbies have been marinated, so they're already a bit cooked.

Crack fresh pepper over everything and serve on fresh bread with a cold one!

green tips

Start from scratch!
Your food will be fresher, healthier and tastier; you know there won't be any chemicals or wasted packaging; and nothing beats the satisfaction of making it yourself.

Be more adventurous!
If you can use whatever's in season, in the pantry or the fridge, you'll waste a lot less time and food - and the best discoveries often come by accident!

Enjoy local specialties!
Enjoy the best of your area - if you live in a region that's well-known for a certain ingredient or specialty, why not celebrate that? Of course, we're blessed in Mildura to have so much excellent produce to choose from, but with so much wheat for our bread and grapes for our wine, I sometimes feel we're at Australia's altar!

Stefano's Cafe Bakery
27 Deakin Avenue
Mildura, VIC 3502
Ph: 03 5021 3627
info@stefano.com.au
www.stefano.com.au

Instead of buying flowers for family and friends, why not give them a potted herb garden with their favourite fresh herbs? They won't rot like cut flowers and they'll provide beautiful, fresh-picked herbs and a wonderful aroma all year round. And every time those special people make dinner, they'll think of you!

d'Arry's Verandah Restaurant

Nigel Rich, Peter and Jo Reschke

Sit on the great Aussie verandah and indulge in the traditions of old: a good meal cooked from the heart, a great drop of red and a magnificent view of the d'Arenberg vineyards that stretches for a far as the eye can see. Welcome to d'Arry's Verandah Restaurant. The rocking chair may be gone, but this welcoming Nineteenth-Century homestead, where the tucker's plentiful and the company's always entertaining, still retains its old-fashioned charm and pioneering spirit.

Nigel Rich, Peter and Jo Reschke draw on their extensive experiences abroad, as well as finding inspiration in the best, freshest and greenest food they can find on South Australia's breathtaking Fleurieu Peninsula.

Mad fisherman Nigel loves cooking locally-caught fish. There's always a tube of wasabi and a fresh lime on his boat for a little mid-trawl snack. He also loves his garden, which is the source of many a chutney, pickle and jam.

Peter and Jo have just built a house and are working on the garden - 'big rain tanks, lots of chook poo and some good old-fashioned sweat' - as well as concentrating on their fast growing kids Oliver and Mia. Both agree that giving back to the environment no matter how small is an important step. Simple solutions such as vegetable scraps used as compost and ground coffee used as slug and snail preventatives. 'Doing something right,' says Peter. 'That's what it's all about.'

You guys seem pretty easygoing, how would you describe yourselves?
Jo: Well, we've all got an optimistic take on life and savour it at every opportunity. We're mainly nutty, sometimes serious, occasionally grumpy with a generous smattering of joie-de-vivre.

You seem to get a kick out of the challenge a seasonal menu brings.
Peter: For sure, each season brings its own charm and joy. Winter's for comfort and richness with braises, truffles, root vegetables and citrus peel. Spring's fresh and lively with fresh chèvre, bitter salads and aromatic broths. Summer's bright and refreshing with unfussy seafood, stone fruit and citrussy dressings. Autumn's golden and gentle with aromatic apples and pears, gentle fruit vinegars verjus and grilled white meats.

Do you think this love for the land and seasonality comes through to your customers?
Nigel: When customers step into d'Arry's Verandah Restaurant the setting's warm and welcoming, the service mature and assured, the food honest and real. The view across the vineyard to the Willunga Escarpment always produces a reaction -it's almost like, 'Phew, we've landed!' Our staff love working here and our customers feel that. What really drives us is that smile, that ecstatic roll of the eye, or that moan of delight from our customers. When we see them return again and again, we know we're doing something right - and that's what it's all about.

And are there any special events for customers who just love the place?
Jo: There's an annual regional food and wine event over the long weekend in June - Sea and Vines. d'Arenberg's built a reputation for being one of the best venues for this, offering d'Arenberg wines by the glass, accompanied by restaurant quality entrée-sized dishes and fab entertainment. d'Arry's Verandah Restaurant offers a lavish seafood degustation menu for the weekend. Each dish is

So how else do you keep things fresh and interesting?
Nigel: We dine out together regularly. Good food and wine are our muses, and boy, how they get the creative juices flowing! We devise all our menus together like that, and our friendship, passion and appetite for new things always keep it interesting. Living on the Fleurieu Peninsula provides us with the perfect backyard, full of seasonal diversity both in wine and food. We could go to a different cellar door or producer every week and still not get to the end of them in a lifetime - magic!
Peter: And every Saturday we visit the local Willunga Farmers Market to see what's new and fresh.

Suppliers are such an important part of any restaurant. How do you get on with yours?
Jo: Really well. We've got close working relationships with our local butcher, Ian; green grocer Craig; olive oil producer, Vince; and fishmongers Ange and Mario. We don't have a baker because we make all our bread ourselves, and no candlestick maker 'cos we've got power! We chose to deal with locals so we could see them face-to-face and discuss our needs, not rely on a series of voicemails or e-mails. They can eat our food, we can sample their produce, and together we can pinpoint exactly what we want.

You have a real rapport with your suppliers. Is this important to you and your local approach to your food?
Nigel: Yeah, definitely. Initially, it was about creating a culture more in tune with what's available locally and naturally with the seasons. The true flavour and texture of many of our everyday foods have been compromised by mass-market production techniques. Buying local and smaller production brings real flavour and texture back to our dishes, ultimately delivering a better culinary experience for our diners - and us. There's nothing better than the heady aroma of herbs plucked from just outside the kitchen door or the piquant mist of lime oil pressed from our own thriving trees.

Does this mean you'll go anywhere for good supplies, or are food miles a factor?
Peter: We source a majority of our supplies locally. Supporting smaller producers that care about their produce, picked at the right time and used within its natural life span. We do not, however, settle for inferior produce for the sake of food mile 'brownie points.'

Are there other ways that you're energy efficient?
Jo: Yeah, lots of ways. Being in the country, rainwater is utilised for most of our consumption. Guests love our filtered "sky juice."

> We recycle as much as we can and we compost all vegetation scraps for our gardens. We even use old coffee grounds as snail and slug preventatives too.

So in the grand scheme of things, how important is it to buy organic food?
Nigel: There's much to be said for organic food production and its benefits to human health, as well as the sustainability of our precious Earth. There has to be a middle ground where we start to incorporate both systems of thought with an overall basis on global consciousness.

You've described your style as honest and from the heart. Has anyone influenced this style?
Peter: The great South Australian chef Peter Jarmer was a mentor and guiding influence for both Nigel and I. I've got fond memories of helping my grandma, who was a stalwart of the South Australian Country Women's Association, and my mum, who was a domestic goddess in her own right, to make cakes, biscuits and slices... the smell of baking butter and vanilla as the timer ticked, the puff of toasty steam as the oven opened.
Jo: My parents were avid disciples of Bacchus. There was a shelf of well-loved cook books in the kitchen, like Tess Malos' Greek Cookery; Simca's Cuisine; The Greta Anna Cookbook; and even Don Dunstan's classic Seventies South Australian cookery bible, The Green & Gold.

After all the food related reality shows we've had on TV do you think anyone can have a go at running a business like yours?
Jo: Anyone can have a go, but not everyone will succeed. It's like any industry: you need to be familiar with the ugly underbelly as well as the glossy pelt of the beast, and know that they're one and the same. You need to value, as well as be prepared to perform, every single job, for it to be a success.

Venue

With its breathtaking views of the Willunga Escarpment, a lush green vineyard in spring and brilliant golds and ambers in autumn, you're blown away from the moment you step through the doors of d'Arry's Verandah Restaurant. Where the ocean meets the vineyard, d'Arry's Verandah Restaurant is an easy-going, relaxing place to enjoy your McLaren Vale tour and drink in all the sights and tastes this world-famous wine region has to offer. Jo, Peter and Nigel's approach to great tucker is keeping it simple, fresh and of the best quality. They're always happy to answer questions on produce and how food is prepared to interested guests. With their close working relationships with local farmers and fishermen, their knowledge of all the ingredients is intimate and extensive: straight from the farmer's gate - and mouth - to you!

Nestled in the beautiful Fleurieu Peninsula, d'Arry's Verandah Restaurant adjoins the d'Arenberg cellar door, and with a extensive wine list to accompany its excellent fare and warm, welcoming service, it's a green dining experience you won't forget. d'Arry's Verandah Restaurant also caters for weddings, parties and just about any time you feel like taking a break from the maddening crowd and enjoying the simple things life has to offer. They're often the best, as Jo, Peter and Nigel will attest!

While they're modest about their achievements, they enjoy a swag of some of country's top hospitality awards and accolades, including Best Winery Restaurant in South Australia 2005, 2006 and 2008; Wine and Spirits Magazine's Best Australian Dining Experience in 2006; and praised by The Weekend Australian as one of Australia's Top Fifty Restaurants in 2009.

d'Arry's Verandah Restaurant is open every day for lunch from 12pm. It's closed for a couple of weeks during winter to allow the team to give their beloved homestead a little TLC, and to discover new green food pleasures for you to enjoy.

Food and Ingredients

'The food we love to cook, and our emphasis at d'Arry's Verandah Restaurant,' says Jo, 'is largely based on what we can see is fresh from the grounds and producers around us. We're in a prime spot up on our little hill to keep in touch with the seasons.'

Working with local suppliers has proved a winning formula, especially a new experiment with locally produced Dorper lambs bred on the d'Arenberg Estate. The Dorper is a South African breed, introduced about thirteen years ago. Peter and Nigel have entered a brave new world of production by overseeing the entire process from slaughter, butchering and utilisation of the whole beast. Rather than just ordering the cuts they want, this hands-on experience has allowed for the creation of a Dorper Lamb feature menu, which includes an entrée of Bresaola of Dorper Lamb with White Anchovy and Parsley Salad; followed by Slow Braised Tomato and Rosemary Dorper Lamb with Soft Polenta and Blistered Truss Tomatoes.

d'Arry's Verandah Restaurant boasts a menu for every season, but of everything they enjoy, the one thing Nigel, Jo and Peter love to cook and eat most is duck. Confit Duck Leg and Seared Breast with Parsnip and Jerusalem Artichoke Smash or an Amuse Bouche of Duck Broth with Parmesan Foam are some of their favourites. Nigel and Peter pair their duck dishes with root vegetables and a pinot noir and duck jus reduction. A shaving of fresh in-season truffle paired with a wonderful d'Arenberg pinot sounds like heaven!

Seafood's another must-have on the menu, given Nigel's passion for fishing. d'Arry's Verandah Restaurant offers three or four seafood dishes, including whatever he's managed to catch that day, or South Australian Pacific oysters. Because Peter, Jo and Nigel all have their preference on how the oysters should be prepared, Nigel just serves them all three ways - 'Mainly because Jo hates to choose and prefers one of everything,' he laughs. In a serving of six oysters, two are left natural with a wedge of fresh lime from their own lime trees on the side as an option, two natural with something fresh and lively like coriander - again from their garden - and wakame salad with a ponzu dressing, two baked gently and topped with ginger foam and finger lime. The squid and fish we source from our local fisherman' says Nigel 'are sweet and tender. The lapis blue around the eyes of the squid says it all: fresh, fresh, fresh!'

Beetroot Cake with Hindmarsh Valley Goat Curd Dumpling

serves six to eight

This unusual and delightful cake highlights the sweetness of beetroot and red onion, treating them as fruits rather than vegetables, and pairing them with pomegranate molasses and orange zest. Deep fried quenelles (or small balls) of goat curd provide a gentle contrast. If you can't get goat curd, try buffalo mozzarella bocconcini, and skip the quenelle making process. If you don't have pomegranate molasses, you can use vincotto, a rich, sticky balsamic vinegar.

ingredients

Beetroot Cake
1kg beetroot
½ red onion, finely sliced
zest of 1 orange
150ml pomegranate molasses or vincotto
salt and pepper
100ml extra virgin olive oil
2 tablespoons or 1 ice cream scoop, dipped in hot water
1 log tin
1 mandolin
1 cream charger

Dumplings
200ml soda water
150g rice flour
250g Hindmarsh Valley goat curd, shaped into quenelles

Beetroot Foam
250ml beetroot juice
1 sheet gelatine

method

Beetroot Cake
Line log tin with baking paper and preheat oven to 150°C. Peel beetroot and slice very thinly on mandolin. Line base of log tin with beetroot, then sprinkle with onion, salt, pepper, orange zest, molasses and a little extra virgin olive oil.

Continue to build up all layers until all beetroot is finished. Cover log tin with baking paper and then with foil. Bake for 50 minutes or until cooked. Check by inserting a skewer into cake centre. It should penetrate easily.

Cool, then place in fridge overnight with a weight on top that evenly distributes pressure - roughly the weight of a plastic wrapped brick. Turn out and carefully cut into 5cm square slices.

Dumplings Method
Mix rice flour and soda water to make a smooth batter. Make quenelles by using taking two dessert spoons dipped in clean hot water - don't dry the spoon, it needs to be wet. Scoop the mixture and roll it on the side of the curd container or mixing bowl to form an egg shape. Slide it off with the other spoon into some dry rice flour, then quickly dip into batter.

Clean spoons in hot water and repeat until all quenelles are made, floured and battered. If you'd prefer the easy option, just use an ice cream scoop, but remember to use it with the warm water. Shake off excess batter and deep fry till lightly coloured.

Drain on kitchen paper.

Beetroot Foam
Dissolve gelatine in warm beetroot juice, then cool and place in cream charger - you'll need a cream charger that uses compressed gas to make the foam frothy.

Serve beetroot cake with goat cheese dumplings on top and a dash of foam. Garnish with rocket.

d'Arry's Verandah Restaurant
Osborn Road
McLaren Vale, SA, 5171
Ph: 08 8329 4848
darrys@darenberg.com.au
www.darrysverandah.com.au

The Brasserie at Hilton Adelaide

Dennis Leslie

Travelling the world on a formative tour of kitchens from Europe to Asia and all points in-between, Dennis Leslie dreamt of home. Adelaide's his hometown, but if you wonder where his heart is, it's right in the kitchens of Hilton Adelaide, South Australia's premier luxury hotel. Beginning with a hospitality traineeship in 1996, Dennis worked his way around the hotel's many departments before being inspired to take up the knives by local Adelaide legends Simon Bryant of ABC TV's The Cook and The Chef (with famed gastronome Maggie Beer) and Cheong Liew of the venerable Grange Restaurant.

After several TAFE qualifications and moving up from housekeeping intern to Hilton Adelaide's Executive Chef, overseeing thirty-three staff and South Australia's largest catering and room service operations, Dennis has found the perfect place to hang his toque: The Brasserie at Hilton Adelaide. His immense pride in his Filipino heritage is matched by his deep concern for the environment and passion for South Australian food and wine, spearheading the Seriously South Australian program with his mentor and mate Simon to encourage the use of South Australian produce. But just as his enthusiasm shines through in every dish, Dennis loves interacting with his diners, to share stories, recipes, ideas and a laugh. 'Hey, I might be serious about food and South Australia,' he says, 'but that doesn't mean it isn't seriously fun!'

Who's been the greatest culinary influence on you?
Oh, definitely Simon, by far. He taught me how to cook right from the start, and he's continued to be a good friend and great mentor. I've learnt so much from so many great chefs, but none greater than Simon. And my mum!

How has South Australia's food culture changed since you donned the toque?
[laughs] Heaps! My mum Violet is Filipino and she cooks with great ingredients like fish sauce, fish paste, dried and pickled fish - stuff my friends growing up would never go near, let alone try. Now, of course, they can't get enough of them. I remember how hard it was getting that stuff growing up, and now, wandering the markets, it's fantastic to see so many shopping bags filled with interesting and exotic ingredients, or seeing all the Asian restaurants in Gouger Street (Adelaide's famed "eat street" and gateway to Chinatown, just around the corner from the Adelaide Central Markets) so full and buzzing. It's just wonderful to see how adventurous people are with the things they'll try, and how that changes what they cook and enjoy at home. There's a whole new generation of young cooks who enjoy so much more variety and choice than we ever did, and more than that, it's through enjoying what other people and cultures enjoy that you can come closer to understanding them, and each other. Multiculturalism hasn't just enriched Australian cuisine, it's enriched Australian society. And we're all much better fed and tolerant for it, I hope!

What are some of the most adventurous foods you've eaten?
It would have to be the Philippines. I ate things like chicken intestines, barbecued congealed pigs' blood - even a real delicacy called balut, which is a nearly developed duck embryo that's boiled and eaten in the shell. It was... interesting. Mind you, I also had some amazingly tasty dishes, like the best suckling pig and sisig, which is a more-ish sizzling hot plate of boiled and chopped pig ears and cheeks seasoned with vinegar, kalamansi (or Filipino citrus) juice, chopped onions and chicken livers. I'd really like to try lots of other unusual or bizarre foods for the experience and education, like, say, Korean live baby octopus sashimi, where you have to wrap the live octopus on a stick and chomp it down before its tentacles strangle you from the inside of your throat. Maybe that'll be my last meal? [laughs]

How about organic food?
Look, I love organic food and I try to use it wherever possible, but it can be difficult to use it consistently or cost-effectively.

How important are food miles?
Absolutely important - they're very high on our priority list. It's not just the environmental benefits of reducing emissions and food miles - many of the cultures and cuisines I've loved and learnt most from celebrate the freshest, locally-grown regional specialties, which is why so many European and Asian cultures have such rich and varied cuisines. And it goes beyond that regionality to bigger issues, like sustainability and ethicality, the hallmarks of good green food.

So what influences your produce selection and menu creation?
Obviously, we're a business, so we have to take our customers' tastes and the bottom line into account, but beyond that, I'm guided by what's in season and what's best at any particular time. You could call me a bit of a hunter-gatherer, though I do a lot of that foraging by phone, ringing around our wonderful suppliers and finding what the best ingredients to use are. I like to be as closely involved as possible, forging close relationships with our suppliers, going out and seeing what they do, and making sure that we recognise their dedication and passion, whether through offering diners the provenance of their meal on the menu - we include where the ingredients have come from and who produces them next to the dish description - as well as the work we've been doing with Seriously South Australian, which celebrates South Australian produce and producers.

Why are you so committed to South Australian produce and producers?
It sounds corny but although I've been round the world, sampling some amazing delights and discovering some great ingredients, I always dreamt of home, and especially the Adelaide Central Markets. We're so lucky in South Australia to have such a wide and varied range of fresh, local ingredients, and even more lucky that we've got such great relationships with our suppliers.

The best thing about using South Australian produce is that it not only supports the local community, it means that diners who love the good green food or interesting ingredients we use can go straight to the Markets and get it themselves.

It's great for us, for our suppliers and producers, for our clientele, and - if they start using those ingredients and teaching their kids to cook and appreciate local ingredients - future generations: economically, culturally and ecologically.

What other green measures have you adopted or implemented?

Hilton Worldwide as a whole - and it's a big whole! - has adopted a more environmentally conscious approach to its operations. In Adelaide, we call it the We Care Program. It implements quantifiable measures that consider things such as water consumption, food recycling, energy usage, waste recycling and water recycling and more. Hilton Adelaide and Hilton Worldwide are very passionate about We Care and there's regular meetings held to discuss monthly consumption and waste results, and, more importantly, ways of improving those results.

We've built an internal database that's accessible through our intranet with which we share green ideas

with other Hiltons around the world to make our guests' stay as comfortable, fun and unharmful to the environment as possible

What's the future got in store for The Brasserie?

I'd love to be known for the passion and knowledge we bring to our diners about our produce, vision and most importantly, food. I'd love people from all over Australia and the world to experience everything South Australia's got to offer - at the table! I'd love to have a bar where people could sit and watch the chefs cooking right in front of them, while they're eating - I love watching good chefs in action while they prepare my meal: you get entertainment, education, and a great meal!

Venue

Long considered one of Australia's food and wine capitals, Adelaide boasts some of the country's best and best known restaurants and vineyards. The Brasserie at Hilton Adelaide is a worthy addition to that illustrious company. Part of Hilton Adelaide, one of Adelaide's best and best-known luxury hotels, The Brasserie's a stylish and casual rendezvous for city shoppers, tourists and locals alike. With a warm Adelaide welcome and the sleek, stylish decor that won Hilton Adelaide the 2007 Australian Hotel Association Awards' Best Deluxe Accommodation Award, The Brasserie has something for everyone. The warm and friendly staff take your enjoyment seriously.

How many major hotel chains with over 3500 hotels in over 70 countries would consider, much less implement, major groundbreaking environmental initiatives like *We Care* to drastically reduce food miles, energy and water usage and food wastage, as Hilton has done? Achievements such as reducing their water usage by 23%, gas by 12%, electricity by 7% and non-biodegradable landfill waste by 10% have won Hilton Adelaide a swathe of very deserved awards, including the Best Environmental Practice Award from the Australian Hotels Association two years' running and the Qantas Award for Excellence in Sustainable Tourism. With Dennis' enthusiastic support, Hilton Adelaide also successfully lobbied to change South Australia's food donation laws, helping pass the Civil Liability (Food Donors and Distributors) Amendment Act 2008, enabling hotels, restaurants and caterers to more freely donate to South Australia's homeless and needy the thousands of tonnes of edible food that would have otherwise been thrown away.

That commitment to ethically, sustainably and locally-sourced and produced green food is championed by Dennis and his team at The Brasserie, with an emphasis on the best fresh and native South Australian produce - so obviously and proudly reflected in the Seriously South Australian initiative which brings together chefs, provedores, growers and suppliers to celebrate everything South Australia has to offer, from the vineyards of the Barossa Valley and McLaren Vale to the olive groves and coastal regions of the Eyre Peninsula and Kangaroo Island, using a cooking style which has been carefully developed to respect and promote the State's beautiful flavours... simple, fresh and unpretentious.

If that little taste just isn't enough, you can join Dennis on tasty tours of the Adelaide Central Markets, where you'll get to see that wonderful abundance and meet some of the producers, growers, provedores and suppliers with whom Dennis works so closely; and exclusive cooking classes with Dennis himself, where you get to feast on an unforgettable meal prepared right in front of you as you enjoy a chat over a glass or three of wonderful matching South Australian wines.

Food and Ingredients

From Adelaide's best brekkie spread to The Seriously South Australian Lunch Buffet, featuring the best South Australia has to offer, from Fresh West Coast Oysters, Dukkah-Crusted Roast Pumpkin, Asparagus and Fetta Frittata, Coriander-Rubbed Rack of Lamb,; or just coffee and freshly in-house baked dessert delights like Chocolate Soufflé Cake, Mini Lemon Curd Tarts and a dangerously delish pâtisserie assortment, The Brasserie's a wonder to see, and the place to be seen.

Dinner continues that seriously South Australian pride, with an extensive and adventurous menu with à la carte that proudly proclaim their inspiration and provenance. 'We love letting our diners know who's responsible for what they're eating,' says Dennis proudly. 'It's a big part of being Seriously South Australian to celebrate South Australian ingredients and the green food pioneers who've dedicated their lives to bringing South Australians and all Australians the very best ethical, sustainable and local green food.'

Like The Brasserie's gourmet take on South Australia's Heritage Icon, the pie floater: Maggie Beer, a rich and hearty porcini mushroom and pâté pie with fresh-picked green pea soup, candied tomato and grape mustard; or Gawler River Heavenly Spiced Quail, from Liz Barnes' free range game farm in the lush Barossa Valley, with Wiech's egg noodle, still made to a third-generation secret recipe faithfully passed from mother to daughter, and Asian vegetable pioneer Lieng Heng's prized greens. For something more substantial, you can't beat Berkshire Gold, a luscious palm sugar, soy and lemongrass glazed confit pork belly straight from Colin and Joy Lienert's free range heritage breed farm, with onion purée and Outback Pride Muntrie Jam; or Dennis' signature dish, the stunning Outback Pride Pepper Berry and Bush Tomato-Rubbed Macro Meats Kangaroo Saddle with Warrigal Green and Muntries, Crispy Saltbush and Quandong and Desert Lime Glaze. 'We source all our native ingredients from the wonderful Mike and Gail Quarmby of Reedy Creek in South Australia's South East, who propagate and supply edible native plants to remote Indigenous communities to preserve ancient traditions and support renewable and sustainable bush food industries run and owned by their Indigenous partners, rightly called "Outback Pride."' Check out their website for stockist information or purchase online (www.outbackpride.com.au). And if you think the name's a mouthful, just wait till you try it!

Everything's matched with "seriously South Australian" sommelier Atef's personal selections, who's always happy to share his extensive knowledge of South Australia's world-famous vintages to find the right wine or boutique beer for the dish and occasion from Hilton Adelaide's vast cellar. And the chef - you know who - loves being complimented and chatting about his love of Seriously South Australian produce and producers, showcased every two months in special South Australian regional specials.

Pepper Berry and Bush Tomato-Rubbed Kangaroo Saddle with Warrigal Greens and Muntries, Crispy Saltbush and Quandong and Desert Lime Glaze

serves four as a main

ingredients

Outback Pride Pepper Berry and Bush Tomato Rub
¼ cup bush tomato, crushed
¼ cup coriander seeds
2 tablespoons ground pepper leaf
2 tablespoons fennel seeds
1 tablespoon ground pepper berries
2 teaspoons ground lemon myrtle
Murray River salt flakes

Quandong and Desert Lime Glaze
600ml freshly-squeezed orange juice
1 cup quandong halves
4 desert limes, skin kept on
5 star anise

Crispy Salt Bush
1 cup saltbush leaves
2 egg whites
½ cup organic cornstarch
2 cups olive oil

Macro Meats Kangaroo
4 kangaroo saddles (about 750g)
3 tablespoons olive oil

Warrigal Greens and Muntrie Berries
100ml lemon juice (from half a lemon, about 1/3 cup)
100g Warrigal Greens, about a handful
½ cup muntrie berries
1 tablespoon olive oil

method

Pepper Berry and Bush Tomato Rub
Blend all ingredients together in a spice grinder or mortar and pestle, then season liberally with Murray River Basin salt.

Quandong and Desert Lime Glaze
Add star anise to orange juice and slowly bring to boil. Reduce Glaze by half and add dried quandong leaves. Halve desert limes with skins on then add to Glaze. Keep warm on low heat and reserve.

Crispy Salt Bush
Wash and dry salt bush leaves. Separate egg yolks, then beat whites in mixing bowl until fluffy. Reserve. Put cornstarch on a plate and roll salt bush leaves in cornstarch until evenly coated. Shake off excess, then dip into egg whites. Heat oil in a deep frypan until hot but not smoking, then fry saltbush until crispy or golden. Drain on kitchen paper and reserve.

Kangaroo
Rinse kangaroo then pat dry. Marinate kangaroo steak with 2 tablespoons of olive oil for ten minutes - because it's so lean, it needs the oil to avoid drying out. Put some Pepper Berry and Bush Tomato Rub on plate and roll kangaroo pieces in Rub until evenly coated. Shake off excess. Discard any Rub on plate; any Rub still in mixing bowl that hasn't touched raw meat can be stored in an airtight container in pantry for up to 1 month.

In a very hot fry pan or barbecue grill, cook kangaroo with 1 tablespoon olive oil for 1 to 1.5 minutes a side until browned all over - it should be on the rare side of medium-rare. Lightly wrap in foil to catch any juices and rest in warm place for at least 1 minute.

Warrigal Greens and Muntree Berries
Blanch Warrigal greens in hot water for 1 minute, then rinse in cold water to remove any oxalic acid. Quickly heat olive oil in frypan to medium heat. Add muntrie berries quickly followed by Warrigal greens. Wilt greens in pan for 30 seconds, then deglaze with lemon juice to make a muntrie sauce. Remove from heat and serve immediately.

To serve, place wilted Warrigal Greens in centre of plates. Slice each kangaroo saddle into 4 or 5 slices across the grain and place slices over Warrigal Greens and Muntrie Berries. Spoon over Quandong and Desert Lime Glaze over kangaroo. Garnish with Crispy Salt Bush leaves then pour over residual de-glazed muntrie sauce from pan.

The Brasserie
Hilton Adelaide
233 Victoria Square
Adelaide SA 5000
Ph: 08 8237 0697
brasserie.adelaide@hilton.com
www.thebrasserie.com.au

The Source Restaurant at Mona

Philippe Leban

After long experience and countless awards at some of the best restaurants in Sydney, Paris and Shanghai, where he won accolades such as Condé Nast Traveler's 100 Hot List Tables 2008, Shanghai's Best New Restaurant 2009, and the American Academy of Hospitality Sciences' Five Star Diamond Award for being one of Asia's Best Chefs in 2009, Philippe Leban took the food world by surprise. He left his prestigious position as Head Chef at Hamilton House on Shanghai's glittering Bund for tiny Tasmania. What could he have been thinking?

But such accolades, while coveted and cherished, are not the only reason the accomplished and warm Philippe cooks. 'I loved my time in Shanghai, but the lure of Tasmania was too great,' he says. 'Everyone talks about how brilliant Tasmanian produce is, and I wanted to be somewhere where I could really explore the produce of a place and push myself further as a chef, using only locally-sourced, in-season ingredients. The real surprise for me was how amazing Mona was - I mean, I'd heard lots of good things, but I can't tell you how lucky I feel, finding exactly what I was looking for, in such a cool, beautiful place!'

The site is on the banks of the Derwent River just outside central Hobart. It was originally named Moorilla, meaning "rock on the water," by the urbane arts benefactor and viticulture pioneer Claudio Alcorso, in 1958, and was one of Tasmania's oldest wine estates. Now, as Mona, it's one of Australia's most exciting and innovative art, architecture, food and wine destinations, home to the award-winning Moorilla Refined Wines; cult boutique beer Moo Brew; Australia's largest private art museum, the Museum of Old and New Art; the stunningly avant-garde Mona Pavilions retreats; and the world-class, locally-sourced temptations of Philippe's ever-changing, always exciting menu at The Source Restaurant.

You say you came to Mona for a closer relationship to the land, its produce and a local community of producers - the same kind of green food culture you found in France and Japan. Is that kind of food culture possible here in Australia?
Why not? I mean, yes, my parents were very much into self-sustainability and they had their own veggie patch and chickens and ducks, but so did a lot of people then - I mean, it wasn't so much being French as, say, the influence of that old sit-com, The Good Life - remember that, with Felicity Kendall? I think a lot of people like my parents became more interested in food and a more self-sustainable lifestyle, and I was definitely influenced by that, obviously! [laughs]

They didn't do anything fancy - it was the Seventies, after all [laughs] - but it was good and honest and most importantly, fresh. They knew good food and instilled that passion in us, and we knew exactly where it came from and what the animals were fed and how they were treated because we helped out, so it really developed my relationship with food and how it should be grown and treated.

Having seen the value of having that personal relationship with food in my professional life, and seeing how much more information and how much more interest there is in food and ingredients today, I'm starting to think that it's "back to the future:" that more and more people are starting to realise that what we used to do with food - raising it ourselves, eating it in season, slow-cooking, respecting tradition, sharing in the pleasures of cooking and eating and drinking together - are the way of the future, and more and more people are saying they've had enough of over-processed, poorly produced "factory food:" that they want to know more about what they're eating, where it came from, how it was produced. I love being able to tell diners that 'this duck comes from that farm, I know the farmer

who raises them, if you like, you can go out and meet him and see his farm and see exactly where your dinner came from and how it's been cared for.'

Just as I found in France or Japan, I hope that new-found enthusiasm and eagerness to learn and know more will become a part of Australia's very vibrant, very inclusive food culture.

Has that new hunger for tradition and information changed people's shopping and dining habits?
Definitely. I see people's attitudes changing every day. With all the information available in the media and internet, you can see where food comes from, how it's caught or produced, and you really have no excuse claiming ignorance. For example, people now know that a lot of cheap imported fish is often illegally poached from polluted waters, and they'd much rather have their fish sustainably line-caught from local waters - after all, you don't have to freeze or process fish that's been caught down the road, and the difference in flavour and freshness is incomparable. People are excited about seeing beautiful, glossy fish that was alive only hours earlier, and they love eating it. I think as more chefs and restaurateurs take a leadership role in using and serving only ethically, locally and sustainably-sourced green food, a whole new Green Food Generation of conscientious diners and shoppers will rise up, for everyone - and the environment's - benefit, and people will seek to make the same ethical decisions in their own shopping and cooking - if only to recapture the freshness and flavour of the green food they've enjoyed at The Source Restaurant.

Unfortunately, changing attitudes are one thing; the real agent for change is action. But the world's insatiable appetite for seafood is devastating. We need to understand, not just as a race, but as a global community, that we can't continue to trawl indiscriminately, hoovering entire marine ecosystems into mile-long nets - fish, most of which aren't edible; dolphins and whales; shellfish; and everything in between, through all stratas of the food chain - without dire and devastating consequences.

Basically, there's ample evidence to suggest that by 2050, there'll be no wild fish in the seas. How scary is that?

I mean, the blue-fin tuna, one of the greatest fish in the sea, is now threatened with extinction in a few years, and governments continue to play politics about it, based on "commercial demand." I mean, what price extinction? It's one thing to extinct a species, like say, the Tasmanian Tiger, out of ignorance; but to do it when you know the facts? Just unbelievable.

Mona's well-known for its innovative approaches to architecture, culture, viniculture and more. How have you added to that philosophy?
Well, apart from the menu being based on ethical, local and sustainable green food and classical culinary traditions, we're in the process of establishing a ten acre kitchen garden. There'll be small plots dotted around Mona and close by where we'll grow our own vegetables and herbs. We'll sell any surplus at farmers' markets or to other restaurants, depending on production and demand.

Naturally, it means much of our produce will be just-picked fresh, but in addition to drastically reducing our carbon footprint, hopefully it'll showcase just how good correctly-grown and picked produce can be!

Are food miles a big factor in purchasing or sourcing produce?
Absolutely. That's the reason I came - to source as much as I could locally, and work within those opportunities and challenges. Unfortunately, being in a remote State, we can't always source everything locally, which is why we're moving towards growing our own veggies, getting our own chickens, producing our own eggs. Hopefully, one day, we'll become nearly 100% self-sustainable, which means diners would know exactly where their dinner came from, how it was grown and picked, how it was cooked, and who was responsible for it from earth to table. That'd just be amazing...

So how does this locality and seasonality affect your menus?
Well, because I'll be working very closely with Mona's amazing horticultural crew, if they say "the asparagus won't be ready for two weeks," I can plan and tailor the menu to accommodate that. And the best part is that we'll have the best produce at the peak of its seasonal quality, picked in the morning and on people's plates by lunchtime. How fresh is that? And in comparison to imported, out of season or hot-housed asparagus, you'd definitely taste the difference!

Venue
Only fifteen minutes' scenic drive from Tasmania's capital Hobart, Mona, under the leadership and vision of David Walsh, is one of Australia's most exciting food, wine and art destinations. David has created a complete experience that will challenge and tease the senses. He calls it 'a subversive Disneyland for adults.'

The original Roy Grounds-designed homestead is the visitor's entry to the collection. A spiral staircase takes you down into the subterranean galleries that have been filled with masterpieces from Ancient Egypt to Damien Hirst, as well as some of Australia's most talented and edgy artists such as Fiona Hall and Archibald Prize winner Del Kathryn Barton. Pieces from David's personal collection are also included in the Mona Pavilions overlooking the Derwent River.

The bold and elegant Pavilions are dedicated to some of the great Australian architects and artists who've influenced Mona, featuring bespoke Tasmanian-designed and crafted furniture and furnishings by a who's who of international designers. All offer the utmost in sophisticated luxury, including personal 24/7 concierge; state-of-the-art entertainment amenities, including iPod dock and high definition televisions; king-size beds with 400-thread-count pure cotton bedding; under-floor heated bathrooms with spa baths; and access to a sauna, gym and naturally-heated lap pool. And each has a fully stocked wine cellar, featuring Moorilla Wines and Moo Brew beers. Mona regularly hosts events and concerts featuring major Australian and international acts, as well as functions from wine tastings to weddings.

David's enthusiasm extends to brewing the cult range of premium boutique beers, Moo Brew, featuring exclusively-commissioned labels by Australian artist John Kelly. Based on his sculpture series of iconic Australian artist William Dobell's wartime airfield cows, the iconoclastic Pilsner, containing only the highest quality German-style Spalt hops or the naturally cloudy, banana, clove and vanilla-aromatic Hefeweizen - as well as the chocolatey Dark Ale, citrussy Pale Ale and the rich and limited-release Imperial Stout - beautifully complement Moorilla Wines. The Muse and Praxis wines also reflect David's approach to the celebration of life's pleasures and the inevitable tension that drives us - the pursuit of sex and the avoidance of death.

A new underground winery has been built to the highest ecological standards using gravity, underground refrigeration, the harnessing of waste heat and more, to save energy and improve wine quality. Liquid waste collected for treatment in a specially-constructed wetland, naturally filtered along with collected rainwater for irrigation. Solid wastes are combined with The Source Restaurant's kitchen scraps for composting. And solar energy, internal water and electricity usage are monitored to further refine and improve efficiency.

Food and Ingredients

Tasmania's salmon, abalone and other seafood delicacies, black truffles, honey, saffron, wasabi, grass-fed beef, cheese and of course, apples are world-famous, and are some of the reasons Philippe left the bright lights of the world's great capitals.

Extending David's vision of a place where art, food, wine and architecture respectfully complement their environment, and reflecting his own passion for ethically, sustainably and locally-sourced produce, Philippe's menu is at once both elegantly simple and sophisticated, reflecting his parent's passion for food and his desire to self-sustainably grow and serve freshly-picked ingredients that not only delight the palate but preserve the planet. In addition to reducing food kilometres, Philippe has his own interesting take on reducing waste, apart from reducing and composting kitchen scraps.

When shown brewing by-products, he devised an intriguing Beer Wort Risotto, using eschalot, butter and beer wort in place of chicken or vegetable stock. 'It really brings out the wort's natural, nutty, toasty wheat sugars for an unusual and delicious new taste,' he says.

Shouldn't be hard to find a beer match for that, then! Despite his extensive knowledge of classical French cuisine, Philippe much prefers the ingredients to do the talking, preferring simple meals that nod to tradition while offering new tastes, textures and visions for modern diners.

From exotic entrées like Scallops, Herb and Zest Couscous, Almond Milk and Perfumed Tomato to more earthy delights like Hare Terrine with Dried Fruit Compote, Philippe celebrates the richness, freshness and variety of Tasmania's produce. Expansive and sumptuous mains like Wild Line-Caught Fish with Truffled Macaroni, Fois Gras Emulsion and Jus or Duck Breast with Belgian Endive, Salted Caramel Apple and Coffee Sauce beautifully showcase the rugged landscape and perfectly match with the Muse Series Pinot Noir or Chardonnay. Make sure you leave room for Philippe's tempting desserts, such as Brioche Pain Perdu with Perfumed Egg Nog and Milk Ice Cream or Pistachio Panna Cotta, Sour Cherry Coulis and Dark Chocolate - or have them delivered to your Pavilion!

Whatever you enjoy, however long you stay, you can enjoy everything The Source Restaurant and Mona have to offer, knowing that luxury needn't cost - or wreck - the earth.

Broiled Oysters with Seaweed Emulsion and Buckwheat Velouté

serves four

'Velouté is what the great gastronome Carême called one of the four "mother sauces" in French cuisine,' says Philippe. 'It's a rich, white roux sauce made with butter, flour and stock, thickened with cream and egg yolks.' You can find roasted buckwheat tea kernels from any good specialty tea shop, Asian supermarket or health food shop.

When you get your oysters, ask your fishmonger to keep the lids on when he shucks them for you, so you can bake them according to the recipe.

ingredients
12 fresh oysters, lids left on
400ml fish stock
200g sea salt
100g flat parsley leaves
100g cream
80g fresh seaweed
50g good quality salted butter
40g roasted buckwheat tea kernels
1 tablespoon grapeseed oil
cracked black pepper

method
Pre-heat oven to 200°C. In a pot, simmer seaweed in fish stock until tender.

While seaweed's cooking, blanch parsley in salted boiling water for 30 seconds, then refresh in iced water. Drain both parsley and seaweed and shake off excess water. Reserve fish stock for sauce.

In an upright blender, slowly drizzle grapeseed oil while puréeing parsley, seaweed and fish stock. Strain mixture through a fine sieve and keep warm on low heat on stove top.

Put buckwheat kernels into pan, then pour cream over. Bring cream to quickly to a boil and let buckwheat kernels steep in warm cream for 15 minutes, then strain through sieve. Season cream to taste with salt and pepper. Keep hot by returning back to the pot from which it was strained.

Line a tray with a generous amount of coarse sea salt, about 200g. Place oysters on salt so they're securely upright, with lids in place. Place tray in oven for 40 seconds.

Carefully remove lids from oysters over strainer placed in bowl to collect juice. Melt butter in pan and stir in oyster juice. Season with cracked black pepper.

To serve, place oysters on a wire baking rack and cover with seaweed sauce until coated. Divide oysters between four bowls. Pour a little oyster-butter dressing over each oyster.

Froth up buckwheat-infused cream with a hand blender and spoon over each oyster.

green tips

Aim for Self-Sustainability
Veggie patches, no matter how small, are a great way to understand and regulate your food, as well as reduce grocery bills and carbon emissions. And there's no fresher than just picked! In the city, where you mightn't have the yard for it, urban gardening is a really popular movement. Sharing allotments or care of the garden with your neighbours is a great way to create a community vibe in the middle of the urban jungle!

Visit Your Local Producers
Hunting, foraging and gathering by visiting farms where your favourite food's produced isn't just a fun and fascinating way to see where your food's coming from, but an important way of supporting independent growers and local businesses. You can find out more at The Green Pages (www.thegreenpages.com.au), Australia's biggest directory of green businesses.

Be Conscientious
Your shopping choices are the easiest and most direct way you can express your support or disapproval of farming, fishing or production practices. Today with wealth of information on the net and the ease you can find it (like checking out The Green Pages, above), there's really no excuse not to be informed, or to make conscientious, ethical decisions on anything from canned tuna to mandarins.

The Source Restaurant at Mona
655 Main Road
Berriedale TAS 7011
Ph: 03 6277 9900

The FIG Cafés

Lorna and Greer Marns

Sisters Greer and Lorna Marns are the driving force behind The FIG Cafés - an exciting, ethical and expanding business, with two buzzing venues - The Wild Fig in Watermans Bay, Perth and The Naked Fig in Swanbourne, a leisurely twenty five minutes' drive away - and another, The Pickled Fig in Fremantle, on the way.

All these funky, fresh café-restaurants are situated on some of Western Australia's most beautiful coastline, attracting diners from all over the State - and the world!

Having started out in cafés when she was fifteen, artistic Greer went on to do a sign-writing apprenticeship, ran her own sign-writing business and completed a degree in visual arts before returning to hospitality at thirty. Now she drives around in a cute little convertible called FIGaro, complete with customised "THE FIG" number plates. Lorna's first hospitality gig at fourteen was earning a mere five bucks an hour at the local Chinese. By nineteen, she was juggling a university degree and shifts at a busy tavern. Even after working in the field of neurogenetics for years, she continued to manage pubs and cafés by night before joining her sister at The FIG Cafés.

Together with their talented executive chef, Sean Carter, energetic and passionate staff, and the very best local WA produce they can find, these creative and committed sisters have combined art and science to serve up something special!

What do you like cooking?
Greer: We don't get much time to cook these days, so it's a good thing we own cafés or we'd starve! [laughs] Lorna's actually a pretty mean cook. Her Ooey-Gooey chocolate pudding is one of the FIG Cafes' signature dishes.

Who's had the most influence over your cooking?
Lorna: My mum! She gave me the freedom and support to experiment in the kitchen. And when Dad got high blood pressure many years ago, Mum changed our diet to include heaps of beans and veggies. It was very common to have a hearty roast veggie salad for dinner.

What do you like eating?
Lorna: It depends on my mood, but my faves are: scallops - so much better than crayfish; fresh dates; those sticky messy barbecue ribs that just fall off the bone; Chinese mushrooms; ruby red grapefruit juice - I can always find room for another glass; any strong, mouldy cheese - the more it stinks of feet, the smoother it'll be; Mum's moreish Christmas mince pies with brandy butter and Sean's awesome Not So Nude Lamb Shanks, braised lamb shanks with spicy tomato sauce, cous cous and rocket raita salad. Oh, and chocolate always makes me happy! [laughs]

What's the most adventurous or unusual food you've eaten?
Greer: Moose in Alaska… before I became a vegetarian.
Lorna: I nibbled some chicken feet once at dim sum, but why bother? Why would anyone want to eat their feet? Where's the meat? Their feet are quite ugly too. No offence, chickens!

How often do you change your menu and what's your favourite season for food?
Lorna: We change our menus twice a year - in May, getting ready for warm, hearty winter meals; and then October, getting ready for a lighter, colourful summer menu. However, that doesn't stop us taking advantage of the best seasonal produce. Our favourite season would have to be fig season… but of course, we'd have to say that! [laughs]

What influence do you have on the produce used at The FIG Cafés?
Lorna: Although we may know how to cook at home, we understand the real skills lie in our team - our executive chef Sean, our head chefs, our kitchen teams and our managers. It's important to us that our food's healthy and ethically conscious. As long as our team supports these values, the decisions belong to them. Our chefs are very hands-on as far as produce selection goes, but we definitely encourage using free-range, fair trade and locally-grown products.

Do profit or punters determine the provenance and quality of the food you serve?
Lorna: Both! Food quality's a market driven thing. If you've got a reputation for good quality, customers will come. If you don't, they'll just go somewhere else. Then you'll either have to lift your game or shut your doors. Just being a café that doesn't offer chips seems to make a difference. Once customers get over the "no chips?" shock they soon find healthy, delicious alternatives on our menu.

What sort of relationship have you got with your suppliers?
Lorna: We and all our staff try to work with honesty and integrity in all our relationships, including with our suppliers. At the end of the day, as a profitable business, we've got to analyse who can give us the best price, but locality, delivery, quality and consistency are all equally important.

How do your suppliers meet your needs?
Lorna: They're amazing! Finding everything from RSPCA-accredited eggs to great organic tempeh, sourcing local produce and fair trade coffee beans, delivering up to four times a day to ensure freshness and quality…
or when the chef's forgotten something!

What do you think about organic food?
Lorna: It's hard to source, expensive and out-of-reach for many consumers. It'd be great to see it more available and more affordable. We'd like to offer more organic food, but have found the market's generally missing basic fresh food that caters to vegetarians, coeliacs, people with other food allergies or preferences. We try our best to accommodate them, though!

And genetically modified food?
Lorna Being a scientist, I'm undecided, but not against. I think there needs to be further research done to determine any potential health problems, but there's a huge potential for food production and assistance for the Third World. Sean's against it, though.

What's your pet hate about the food industry?
Greer: Food snobs and restaurant critics who've never owned a restaurant. Also those wanky photos in foodie magazines of chefs and managers with serious "blue steel" facial expressions - come on guys, give us a smile!

If you could change one thing about the food you serve, what would it be?
Lorna: To provide food that, as you ate it, actually reduced your calorie consumption. We'd be soooo popular and you could eat and eat and eat … and eat! Everyone would be a winner! [laughs]

How do you keep things fresh and interesting?
Greer: We're always looking for what's new and what the community wants. We started a Curry Night and a Veggo Feast Night. We try to offer things that other places don't. Eating out's about an experience, so we try to satisfy all the senses with live music, funky art on the walls, ocean views, a relaxing ambience, a menu offering vegetarian, vegan and gluten-free options - lots of added extras!

Your food's very green! What other green measures have you implemented at The FIG Cafés?
Greer: We use energy-efficient light globes, recycle as much as we can, and give away our old coffee grinds to gardeners for compost.

We seek local produce and are currently investigating purchasing carbon off-set credits with a view to becoming carbon neutral.

Venue
The Wild Fig Café is on the waterfront at Waterman's Bay, northwest of Perth, Western Australia. The Naked Fig Café overlooks Swanbourne beach-one of Perth's premium Western suburb beaches. Looking out on the glittering edge of the Indian Ocean, both cafés enjoys glorious views and fabulous sunsets. For the early birds who appreciate a sunrise as much as a sunset, The FIG Cafés are open for breakfast from 6.30 am, although more leisurely Sunday brekkies are especially popular.

The Wild Fig opened in December 2000 and The Naked Fig in December 2009. The cafés are home to amusingly-named fresh and delicious food, live music, and a laid-back vibe. As well as using local produce in its dishes, all The FIG Cafés also supports local artists. Funky, vibrant works of art line the walls and local musicians entertain with jazz and smooth soul.

According to the girls, music is the food of love - or something like that! On Tuesdays, you can enjoy the spicy pleasures of curry with the haunting melodies of the sitar; on Wednesday night Veggo Feasts, acoustic jazz-groove guitarist Matthew Bell evokes a silky soul mood.

The FIG Cafés are environmentally and socially conscious. Greer, Lorna and Sean strive to ensure everything is as free-trade, free-range and local as possible.

And those fabulous FIG folk aren't just committed to feeding starving patrons - they also contribute over $5,000 a year in tips from every venue to The Hunger Project, a non-profit organisation dedicated to ending world hunger.

But it's not all earnest and worthy. Greer, Lorna, Sean and everyone at The FIG Cafés reckon you can have a good time too. Their playful menu is testament to their belief that simple, fresh food done right can be as spectacular as the view and the entertainment!

Food and Ingredients

Fresh, ethically and locally-sourced produce form the basis of The FIG Cafés' exciting yet unpretentious cuisine. Sean and his team of passionate chefs constantly experiment to create new and inspiring dishes.

Tuesdays are Curry Nights, with spicy Fire Starters entrées and a selection of The Heat is On mains, like Hot Tongue Curry; the gluten-free Deer Me, with juicy venison pieces in a creamy tomato curry; and the milder Billy, tender mutton in a tomato and mango curry with seasonal vegetables. Other traditional curries are given a uniquely FIG twist: Lamb Korma's made with slow-cooked lamb shanks; and Beef Jalfrezi's spiced up with tender, diced scotch fillet, slow-cooked in a seductive capsicum and tomato curry on a bed of cous cous. Not your average balti!

Wednesdays are Veggo Feasts, dedicated to all things veggie, rooty and leafy.
The freshest, locally-grown produce stars in every dish. Mushrooms, beetroot, rocket, onions, tomatoes, zucchini, olives, eggplant, spinach and herbs are teamed with feta, chèvre, parmesan and Napolitano sauce in a range of light and tasty dishes with names like Pink, succulent oven-roasted beetroot, asparagus and fetta risotto with crisp sweet potato curls; or Wild, a mouth-watering trio of porcini, Swiss brown and button mushrooms in a soft thyme and parsley risotto finished with basil olive oil and a parmesan crisp. The usual suspects - dhal, nachos and chickpeas - are all there, but spiced up the Figgy way!

Breakfasts overlooking the beach are a huge hit. Not just for the view, but Amuesingly, a delightful concoction of toasted muesli, stewed rhubarb and rosewater, toasted nuts, strawberry compote, Athena yoghurt, castilla and poached pear; The Nudie Vegan, a rich spread of grilled asparagus, roast pumpkin, roma tomato, field mushrooms, fresh baby spinach, seasoned red beans and pumpkin rye toast; and Naked South of the Border, a naughty-but-very-nice red beans, chorizo and baby spinach in a spicy tomato sauce topped with creamy shaved cheddar, and served with tomato-infused casalinga.

Ooey Gooey with Honey Balsamic Figs

serves four

Lorna's signature dessert may have had many different accompaniments, including these divine honey balsamic figs, but it never changes - and Greer assures us, never will. "Nothing beats the look on a customer's face when they break the crust of their 'Gooey with their spoon and the warm rich centre spills all over the plate," she says. "It's as close to heaven as we can offer."

ingredients

Ooey Gooey
500g cooking chocolate (minimum 55% cocoa)
500g unsalted butter, cubed
300g caster sugar
200g flour
8 whole eggs
extra butter and caster sugar for lining moulds
16 small squares of greaseproof paper
16 metal moulds for the Ooey Gooeys
chocolate sauce, to serve
icing sugar, to serve
vanilla ice cream, to serve
hot chocolate powder, to serve

Honey Balsamic Figs
8 figs, quartered
1 tablespoon balsamic vinegar
1 tablespoon brown sugar
1 tablespoon honey

method

Combine quartered figs, balsamic vinegar, brown sugar and honey in a small bowl for at least an hour. Pre-heat oven to 180°C.

Line all moulds with butter, then half-fill one mould with caster sugar and shake vigorously. Tip remaining sugar into next greased mould, then turn the first mould upside down and bang on bench top to release any surplus sugar. Continue process until all moulds are greased and sugared.

Melt chocolate and butter over a double boiler on low heat, stirring often until completely softened. Remove from heat and allow to cool slightly - but make sure you keep it above room temperature so it doesn't set! You can do this by just popping a plate or cover over the chocolate.

Cream sugar and eggs until pale in colour. Slowly sift flour into creamed eggs, folding gently until no lumps remain. Fold chocolate into eggs one ladle at a time. Place a small square of greaseproof paper into moulds and ladle in gooey mix until 1cm below rim. Place moulds 5cm apart on baking tray and cook for approximately 20 minutes, or until cooked. Using a butter knife, lift Ooey Gooeys away from the mould and tip out onto a plate.

To serve, top the Ooey Gooey with chocolate sauce and icing sugar. Arrange honey balsamic figs around plate and serve with good vanilla ice cream and a generous dusting of hot chocolate powder.

green tip

It's all about being aware and informed. Seek answers for questions like:
What's possible?
What fits with my values?
What's the impact?
What's available?
Is there an alternative?

The Wild Fig Café
33 West Coast Drive
Watermans Bay WA 6020
Ph: 08 9246 9222
www.thefig.com.au

The Naked Fig Café
278 Marine Parade
Swanbourne WA 6010
Ph: 08 9384 1222
www.thefig.com.au

Green Food Glossary

Additives
Substances added to food in order to preserve, flavour, or improve its taste and/or appearance. While some food additives are natural and have been used for centuries (such as vinegar for pickling), modern additives are often chemicals in processed food which enhance flavour (like MSG) or colour it.

Aquaculture
Underwater agriculture; the cultivation of aquatic animals or plants, such as fish and shellfish, by people or corporations who own the harvestable product, often involving the capture of the eggs or young of a species from wild sources.

Bycatch
Unwanted marine creatures, most of which are discarded at sea, that are caught in the nets while fishing for another species.

Carbon diet
In order to go on a carbon diet, a person or business must first measure its carbon footprint (the amount of greenhouse gases released by through day-to-day activities including operating all of our modern technology) and then cut out its most wasteful practices first.

Carbon tax
A charge on the emissions caused by the burning of coal, gas and oil, aimed at reducing the production of carbon dioxide (the chief greenhouse gas).

Pelagic fish
Fish that live in the open ocean at or near the water's surface but remain relatively close to the coast (such as mackerel, anchovies and sardines).

Compost
The result of a process whereby organic waste (from food, paper and the yard) decomposes naturally and to become a product rich in minerals and ideal for gardening and farming.

Crop dusting
The application of pesticides to plants by a low-flying plane.

Demersal fish
Fish that live on or near the ocean bottom, often called 'benthic fish', 'groundfish' or 'bottom fish'.

Dredge
A fishing method whereby a bag is dragged behind a vessel to scrape the ocean bottom, usually to catch shellfish. Dredges are often equiped with metal spikes in order to dig up the catch.

Drift net
A large net stretching across many kilometres that drifts in the water, primarily for large-scale commercial fishing purposes.

Eco-friendly
Not harmful to the environment, friendly and supportive of environmental ecology.

Ecosystem
An interconnected and symbiotic grouping of animals, plants, fungi and microorganisms.

Emissions cap
A limit on the amount of greenhouse gases that a company or country can legally emit.

Endangered species
Any species, plant or animal, whose population has dropped so low that they are in danger of becoming extinct.

Energy conservation
Using energy efficiently or prudently saving energy.

Energy efficiency
Technologies and measures employed to reduce the amount of electricity and/or fuel required to provide the same level of energy service (such as powering homes, offices and industries).

Environmentally sustainable
Maintaining the factors and practices that contribute to the quality of environment on a long-term basis

Factory farming
Large-scale industrialised agriculture.

Factory ships
Industrial-style ships used for the large-scale collection and processing of fish.

Fair trade
A social movement advocating fairness in all aspects of food production and distribution, including wages of workers and environmentally sustainable practices.

Feed lots
A plot of ground used to feed farm animals.

Fertilisers
Any substance, such as manure or a chemical compound, that is added to soil or water in order to improve its productivity. Artificial fertilisers are often used in conventional large-scale farming methods, which tend to ravage the soil. Organic methods are extremely environmentally sustainable helping plant growth, reducing waste and reducing the energy usage that usually occurs through the production and distribution of artificial fertilisers.

Fisheries
An established area where fish species are cultivated and caught.

Fossil fuels
Fuel, such as coal, oil and natural gas, that is produced by the decomposition of ancient fossilised plants and animals.

Free-range
Livestock and domestic poultry permitted to graze or forage rather than being confined to a feedlot.

Gill nets
Walls of netting that are usually staked to the sea floor. Fish become entangled or caught by their gills. See also driftnets.

Global warming
Increase in the average temperature of the earth's surface that causes corresponding changes in climate.

GM Genetically Modified
An organism, such as vegetable, whose DNA has been altered by the insertion of a modified gene or a gene from another organism.

Grain-fed
Livestock that have been fed grain throughout their lives. Grain-fed meat is a bad practice both for reasons of animal well-being and for the quality of the meat. Ruminating animals are not supposed to consume grains and their diet has a major influence on the nutritional content of its products.

Grass-fed
Livestock that have eaten only grass or forage throughout their lives. However, some producers do call their meat grass-fed but actually finish the animals on grain for the last 90 to 160 days before slaughter.

Grass-finished
Livestock that have eaten only grass or forage throughout their lives. Grass-finished cattle are fattened on grass only until the day that they are processed.

Grassroots
Local or person-to-person. A typical grassroots effort might include a door-to-door education and survey campaign.

Grazing
The use of grasses and other plants to feed wild or domestic herbivores (such as deer, sheep and cows).

Greenhouse
A building made with translucent light and transparent walls, usually from glass or fibreglass, which is conducive to plant growth.

Greenhouse effect
The process that raises the temperature of air in the lower atmosphere due to heat trapped by greenhouse gases such as carbon dioxide, methane, nitrous oxide, chlorofluorocarbons and ozone.

Groundwater
Water below the earth's surface: the source of water for wells and springs.

Grower
A farmer or cultivator: someone who grows produce (such as beef or honey).

Growth overfishing
the process of catching fish before they are fully grown resulting

Harpooning
A surface method of fishing that requires considerable effort in locating and chasing individual. fish Harpoons are hand-held or fired from a harpoon gun and aimed at high-value fish such as giant tuna and swordfish.

Incinerators
Disposal systems that burn solid waste or other materials and reduce volume of waste.

Insecticides
Substances used to kill insects and prevent infestation of plants and in some cases animails.

Landfill
Disposal area where garbage is piled up and eventually covered with dirt and topsoil.

Local
Local foods refer to food that is locally grown the practice of local consumerism creates self-sustainable local economies lower carbon emissions and often better diets and social accountability within a community.

Long lines
Fishing lines stretching for dozens of miles and baited with hundreds of hooks.

Managed growth
Growth or expansion that is controlled so as not to be harmful.

Organic
Produce that is raised or grown without the use of drugs hormones or synthetic chemicals.

Over-fishing
Fishing beyond the capacity of a population to replace itself through natural reproduction.

Over-grazing
Grazing livestock to the point of damage to the land.

Pastured meat
Livestock that has been raised and allowed to roam in pastures. Sometimes meat is advertised as grass-fed but the cattle stay in feed lots - though they are fed on grass.

Pesticides
A pesticide is a substance or mixture of substances used to kill a pest. A pest can be any organism that corrupts a crop or produce. In farming, pesticides prevent the crop from being corrupted but there are disadvantages to their use which can include toxicity, high carbon emissions and energy usage in production and distribution.

Pollution-prevention
Waste collected after the consumer has used and disposed of it e.g. the wrapper from an eaten candy bar.

Processed
Prepared or converted from a natural state by subjecting to a special process.

Producer
Producers produce the food or food products which is then sold.

Recycling
System of collecting sorting and reprocessing old material into usable raw materials.

Reduce
Act of purchasing or consuming less to begin with so as not to have to reuse or recycle later.

Solar energy
Energy derived from sunlight.

Solid waste
Non-liquid, non gaseous category of waste from non-toxic household and commercial sources.

Supplier
Suppliers play a crucial role in the food industry by linking the growers to the buyers. For example supplying restaurants with niche products.

Surface water
Water located above ground e.g. Rivers, lakes.

Tap water
Drinking water monitored and often filtered for protection against contamination and available for public consumption from sources within the home.

Terrior
The combination of contextual characteristics including soil, climate and environment that gives produce its specific flavour. Mostly used in regards to wine.

Trolling
A method of fishing using several lines each hooked and baited which are slowly dragged behind the vessel.

Unprocessed
Not altered from an original or natural state not treated or prepared by a special process.

Whole foods
Are those that are unprocessed and unrefined or processed and refined as little as possible before being consumed They typically do not contain added ingredients such as sugar salt fat or preservatives

Acknowledgments

Also by Hayden Wood:
The Liquid Kitchen: Groovy Drinks
The Liquid Kitchen: Party Drinks
Woody's Liquid Kitchen
Good Wine, Bad Language, Great Vineyards
Beer Nuts
Café Republic of Australia (with Scottie Callaghan)

Published in 2010 by Drink Australia Pty Ltd.

Drink Australia Pty Ltd.
PO Box 873, Newtown NSW 2042, Australia

All rights reserved. No part of this publication may be reproduced, stored in a retrieval system or transmitted in any form or by any means, electronic, mechanical, photocopying, recording or otherwise, without the prior written permission of the publisher.

Green Food Generation is a trademark of Drink Australia Pty Ltd.

A CIP catalogue record for this publication is available from the National Library of Australia.

ISBN: 978-0-9775147-7-9

Text Copyright © 2010, Drink Australia Pty Ltd.
Photographs Copyright © 2010, Drink Australia Pty Ltd.
Design Copyright © 2010, Drink Australia Pty Ltd.

The moral right of the author has been asserted.

Author: Hayden Wood
Graphic Designer / Painter: Esmeralda Wood
Printed by ibook Printing Limited.
Printed in China. Printed 2010.

Some recipes contributed by chefs may require a level of skill and technique of cooking that is above the competency level of some home cooks. It is advised to asses the recipe prior to attempt and when in doubt of your abilities, seek additional support or advise.

As the views and opinions contained within this book come from a collection of food professionals, they may not necessarily be those shared by the author. The context of the book is to share and foster conversation openly over the diner table with a hope to improve the outcome of our precious recourses for future generations.

If you're not in hospitality, volunteer or donate money to help OzHarvest continue its wonderful work - we're putting our money where our mouth is by donating ten percent of all the profits from this book to OzHarvest!

www.drinkaustralia.com.au
www.woodysliquidkitchen.com

Thanks to Esmeralda for her beautiful artworks, which can also be found at www.esmeraldawood.etsy.com

The Harvest	Page 12
Special Chicken	Page 46
Singing Whales	Page 88
Mother Nature	Page 122
The Giving Tree	Page 164

Thank You

To all the farmers, growers, producers and suppliers we met along the way - you really are the unsung heroes of this book and the green food generation.

Thanks Curtis for your meaningful foreword, and thanks to Jodie Gatt, Mario Manabe and all the Stone Foods team for your wonderful support.

Shaun and Willa, thanks for your passionate support of regional restaurants and produce - and good luck with the sleepless nights ahead!

David and Nicole, thanks for showing me such an enviable lifestyle in tune with your community and countryside. And Dave, you're going to need a cocktail list if you're going to get me down more often...

Thank you Miccal and all your hardworking team at Gastronomy - you guys really have a knack for staying cool in the hottest catering kitchen in town!

Molte grazie, Stefano di Pieri, for your generosity, time and energy for green good food in the "Outback Med" and beyond. You really deserve your brother's triumphant organ music to accompany you wherever you go.

Thanks, Alex for introducing me to Eveleigh Farmers' Markets (http://www.eveleighmarket.com.au/farmers.html) - such a wonderful "discovery" right round the corner from home!

Power to you and your vision, Nick and Imogen! There aren't many who'd go to the lengths you have to do what you do, but thank goodness there are, and you're two of 'em!

How can I ever thank you, Ronni, for sharing your passion and vision? And Father Brian, Scott, Carla and everyone at Newtown Mission (http://www.newtownmission.org.au), I'm back for another shift anytime you want me. I mean it!

Selvam and Jo, thanks for teaching me so much about such a wonderful place and culture. And for being as eloquent as the mad but truthful Zieko was profane!

Bravo to Paul and all the Parra boys in the Tardis kitchen for putting in such a grand effort! And thanks to Karen and her goats, P. Marshall and their animals - and all the wonderful producers who made it to the producers' lunch.

Although it was a fleeting visit, merci to Philippe and the Source team for such lovely delicacies and the Moo brews.

To the seriously committed Hilton Adelaide team, including Dennis and Laura who've thrown up such a benchmark for green food and hostelry in Australia - keep up the awesome work!

Thank you, Stefano Manfredi, Brian and Karina Barry and all at Bells at Killcare. The passion you've invested in this wonderful place is why it's the best place to be on the Central Coast.

Thanks Andrew and Lisa for your friendship and support over the years, and Ian Atkinson for your quick wit and dedication to my favourite Hunter Valley restaurant.

To Greer and Lorna, Sean and all the folks in WA who keep it so figgin' real and fresh.

Bender, thanks not just for being so patient in the middle of opening a new restaurant, but being so hilarious - what a total pro, and a great bloke. And thanks, Todd and all the crew at Blue Harvest (http://www.blueharvest.com.au/) for such a great day!

Victor and Jim, two of the hardest working and most effective green food communicators in the business. And now I know why you bring tequila to events!

Merci beaucoup, Louise and Bruno - your delicious duck dish will keep me thinking, especially about slowing down and finding the time to cook it. Somehow, I reckon that'll happen when I'm next in Mullum.
And thanks to everyone at Santos (http://santostrading.com.au/home.html)
and Espresso Botero (http://www.espressobotero.com.au).

Craig, ta for your devotion to bush tucker and taking the time to have a laugh.

Many thanks to Paul and Rache for the most genuine hospitality and good times I've enjoyed. Your wonderful bush tucker Sangrias and tapas kept me going - thanks for making it so good I'll just have to come back!

And to Luke, Nigel, Peter and Jo for such a good green food time in the vale and your wonderfully warped sense of humour, I love it!

To my New Zealand family, scattered across the islands and the sea, I know how hard it can be to catch up, but I was so glad to snatch a few days with Dad and Vivvy. I wish I had more time to fish... but don't I always say that?

To my Australian family, Amalia and Jaime, muchas gracìas for looking after Esmeralda and Zyon while I'm away - we couldn't do it without you.

To my American family - Tom, Reid and the Grand Krew team, thanks for your support and drive. Thank you Bobby for all your support and the generous use of the photo. And Guy, you were partly responsible for inspiring me to take this journey and write this book, and for this - amongst too much else to mention here - I thank you.

And Anthony "Mr Family" Telford - words can't express my gratitude for your "drop everything and go" attitude to the 4am starts and midnight finishes, the freezing mornings and cheap hotels, while we whinged and you kept filming! Thanks for making it so fun and real... and wasn't it so real, hey? Told ya!

Dave Lang, for all the work you're doing behind the scenes to ensure that the Green Food Generation can tell its story to the beat of a new drum, thanks.

Dom and Shyamla, really special thanks for picking this project up, running with it and pulling all the words together in such a short time under such pressure.

And last but by no means least, to my darling Esmeralda and Zyon. Thanks for being so strong and loving and supportive of me for all the time I spend away doing all this stuff. I know it's not easy sometimes and it's your love and strength that keeps me doing what I do. Esmeralda, who's always there to bring everything together so beautifully - your talent and passion humble me to my core, and your love completes me.

Recipe Ingredients Index

anchovy, 86, 96
baking powder, 20
banana leaf, 44
basil, 62
bay leaves, 54, 62, 112
beef, 70
beer, 20
beetroot, 172
beetroot (juice), 172
blachan, 130
bok choy, 130
bread, 86,
bread (sourdough), 36, 162
buckwheat tea kernels, 188
bush tomato, 180
butter, 36, 104, 162, 188
butter (unsalted), 70, 196
cabbage (chinese), 130
capers, 86
capsicum (red), 130
carrots, 54, 70, 112, 130
celery, 54, 70,112
cheese, 20
cheese (Heidi Gruyere), 36
cheese (Parmesan), 54, 86
chervil, 96
chicken, 54
chicken (bones), 54
chickpeas, 146
chilli (birds eye), 130
chilli (jalapeño), 44
chilli (long and red), 120
chilli (powder), 138, 146
chives, 62, 86
chocolate (cooking), 196
chocolate (sauce), 196
cinnamon (stick), 112
clove, 54, 112
Cognac, 112

coriander (bunch or leaves), 112, 120, 130, 138
coriander (powder), 138, 146
coriander (seeds), 154, 180
cornstarch, 180
cream, 188
crocodile, 130
cucumber, 138
cumin (ground), 146
cumin (seeds), 146, 154
curry (leaves), 138, 147
curry (powder), 146
desert limes, 180
dill, 96
duck fat, 112
duck, 112
dukkah, 154
egg (quail), 104
egg, 36, 54, 86, 96, 162, 180, 196
eschalot, 54, 70, 104
fennel (bulb), 62
fennel (seeds), 180
fenugreek (seed), 146
figs, 196
fish, 78
fish, (Atlantic salmon), 62
fish (Barramundi), 138
fish (Kingfish), 96
fish (stock), 188
flour, 20, 54, 70, 196
flour (corn), 130
flour (potato), 130
flour (rice), 172
garam marsala, 146
garlic, 20, 44, 54, 62, 70, 86, 96, 104,112,130, 138, 146, 154
gelatine, 172
ginger, 130, 146, 154
goat curd, 172
ham (double), 36
hazelnuts, 154
herbs (micro), 62

honey, 112, 154, 196
horseradish, 78
hot chocolate powder, 196
ice cream (vanilla bean), 196
jurniper (berries), 112
kangaroo, 180
leek, 54, 86, 96, 112
lemon, 86, 96, 130, 180
lemon (bush), 78
lemon (bush), 78
lemon aspen, 130
lemon myrtle, 180, 154
lentils red, 146
lime, 44, 78, 120, 138
mango, 120
marjoram, 70
mayonnaise (Japanese), 120
milk, 20, 86, 104
mould spores (Camembert), 20
mountain pepper, 154
muntries, 180
mushrooms (Button), 70
mushrooms (Swiss Brown), 86
mustard (Dijon), 36
mustard (seed), 146
oil (garlic), 162
oil (grape seed), 96, 188
oil (olive), 44, 62, 70, 78, 86, 96, 104, 154, 172, 180
oil (peanut), 120
oil (sesame), 130
oil (vegetable), 96, 130, 138, 146
olives (black), 96
olives (Sevillano), 62
onion (brown), 70, 112, 130, 146
onion (red), 138, 172
onion (white), 54
orange (juice), 180
orange (zest), 62, 172
oysters, 188
pancetta, 70
pappadums, 138

parsley, 54, 70, 86, 188
parsnip, 70
pastry (Kadayif), 120
peas, 104
pepper berries, 180
pepper leaf, 180
pepper, 70, 86, 96, 104, 130, 162, 172, 188
peppercorns, 54, 112, 78
pistachio nuts, 154
pomegranate (molasses), 172
prawns, 44, 130
prawns (Green Tiger), 120
quail, 154
quandong, 180
radish (Daikon), 130
rennet, 20
riccotta, 54
rosemary, 112
sage, 70
salt (sea salt flakes), 96
salt, 20, 54, 62, 70, 78, 86, 104,112, 130, 138, 146, 162, 172, 180, 188
saltbush, 180
sambal oelek, 130
sauce (BBQ), 36
sausage (italian pork), 162
seaweed, 188
sesame seeds, 154
shallots, 54, 70, 104
shiso, 62, 78
silverbeet, 96
soda water, 172
soy (sauce), 78
star anise, 112, 180
starter (Camenbert), 20
stock (beef), 70
stock (veal), 104
sugar (brown), 196
sugar (caster), 196
sugar (icing), 196

sugar (palm), 130
sugar (white), 62, 112, 130
tamari, 78
tarragon, 54
tequila, 44
thyme (lemon), 104
thyme, 54, 62, 70, 112
tomato paste, 130
tomato puree, 130
tomato, 112, 62, 146
tumeric (powder), 138, 146
turnip, 70
venison, 104
verjuice, 96
vincotto, 172
vinegar (balsamic), 196
vinegar (sherry), 96
vinegar rice wine, 130
warrigal greens, 180
wasabi, 78, 120
watermelon, 120
wattleseeds, 154
wine (red), 70
wine (Shiraz), 112
wooden skewers, 120
yabbies (fresh-water), 162